ART OF ROME,
ETRURIA, AND MAGNA GRAECIA

ART OF ROME, ETRURIA, AND MAGNA GRAECIA

Text by GERMAN HAFNER

HARRY N. ABRAMS, INC. Publishers NEW YORK

Front end papers:

Trajan's Battle with the Dacians. Marble, height 9′ 9³/₈″. Beginning of second century A.D. On the Arch of Constantine, Rome

Back end papers:

Sacrificial Scene. c. 60 B.C. Villa dei Misteri ("Villa of the Mysteries"), Pompeii

Translated from the German by Ann E. Keep

Standard Book Number: 8109–8022–3
Library of Congress Catalogue Card Number: 71–92911

Copyright 1969 in Germany by
Holle Verlag GmbH, Baden-Baden
All rights reserved. No part of this book may
be reproduced without the written permission of the publishers
Harry N. Abrams, Incorporated, New York
Printed in West Germany. Bound in the Netherlands

Contents

Introduction 6

The Origins: Eighth Century B.C. 13

Sixth Century B.C. 34

Fifth Century B.C. 76

Fourth Century B.C. 110

Third Century B.C. 137

Second Century B.C. 169

First Century B.C. 180

The Age of Augustus (27 B.C.–A.D. 14) 190

First Century A.D. (Early Imperial Period) 203

Second Century A.D. (Middle Imperial Period) 222

Third and Early Fourth Century A.D. (Late Imperial Period) 238

Chronological Tables 253

Map 256

Bibliography 257

Index 260

Photo Credits 264

Introduction

The significance of Greek art is not confined to Greece or the territories settled by Greeks. One of its most important qualities was that it could be exported to other countries and other peoples.

Greek art—its spiritual center located in Athens—spread to Italy, where Rome was to become the political center. The manner of this outflowing is not only of the greatest importance on account of the subsequent development of European art but is also of the greatest interest from the standpoint of the art historian, since we may distinguish three stages or forms in which this influence was transmitted.

The Greeks who lived in the colonial cities of southern Italy and Sicily (Magna Graecia) gave birth to art forms which acquired an idiosyncratic aspect on account of the geographical situation of this area and the diversity of the peoples living in it. The Etruscans exhibit a picture—not to be seen again in this way—of a people which threw itself upon the treasury of Greek artistic forms, imported Greek art, and probably also gave Greek artists opportunities to work in Italy; but which also, through the intensive reworking of alien elements, shaping them and revising them in the light of Italic concepts, created something unmistakably its own. The Romans, on the other hand, afford the equally unique spectacle of a people who rejected decisively and with determination every opportunity of activity in any of the fields of pictorial art, but who did make use of foreign artists' skills where these suited their own requirements. Rome is thus a meeting place of Italic-Etruscan art, Lower Italic Greek art, and lastly of Greek art proper. Here, in the world's new capital city, in the service of Rome, was written the final chapter of their long history: of their fusion and role as the art of the Roman world empire.

FROM THE BEGINNINGS TO THE ROMAN EMPIRE

The complete absorption of Greek art into "Roman" art, which corresponds to the absorption of Greece into the Roman Empire, was part of a general reorientation of the Roman spirit. What made it possible was an event that for the first time opened the Romans' eyes to the aesthetic appeal of Greek art, to which they had hitherto been impervious. In the middle of the Second Punic War, shortly after the Romans had been severely defeated at the Battle of Cannae, and in the very year (211 B.C.) when Hannibal stood before the gates of Rome, M. Claudius Marcellus showed to a crowd of curious onlookers Greek works of art brought to Rome from Syracuse, which he had conquered. This set in motion a wave of enthusiasm among his compatriots, who spent many hours examining the fine statues and paintings, delighting in them, and discussing art and artists with one another (Plutarch, *Marc.,* 21; Livy, 34, 4). Nothing of the kind had been seen in Rome before. Old-fashioned citizens resisted such uninhibited attraction to alien and unnecessary novelties, which in their view could only be an encouragement to idleness; but they were powerless to halt the course of events. "During the Second Punic War, the Muse joined the wild, warlike race of Romulus" (Porcius Licinus).

What had its origins here at the end of the third century B.C. gathered momentum during the following century, when triumphant Roman generals brought back large quantities of Greek statues and paintings from the lands they conquered in Greece and Asia. During this century Rome became the center of artistic life as well as of the political world.

A complete transformation took place, for prior to 211 B.C., if ancient writers are to be believed, Rome presented a completely different picture: the only embellishments of the city were weapons and bloodstained objects seized from the barbarians, since the Romans declared they had other, more urgent, tasks to fulfill (Plutarch, *Marc.*, 21; Strabo, 5, 235). Their numerous hard-won victories over their neighbors yielded no luxurious booty, but more material things, "the cattle of the Volsci, the flocks of the Sabines, the chariots of the Gauls, or the weapons of the Samnites" (P. Annaeus Florus, *Epitome of Roman History*, I, 18). And even where they had the opportunity to carry off works of art they did not do so, since they preferred their vanquished enemies rather than themselves to be corrupted by the pernicious influences emanating from them; if the conquered took pleasure in such objects, they would in some measure be diverted from gathering strength to make further trouble for the Romans (Cicero, *In C. Verrem*, II, 4, 40).

It is obvious, then, that the Romans, who with exemplary single-mindedness and logic directed their entire strength to the task of securing and expanding their state, had no time to become interested in things so frivolous as works of art. Indeed, the Romans evidently had a deeply ingrained antipathy to pictorial art; enthusiasm for it, let alone actually indulging in it, was considered alien to the Roman way of life; Cato's reaction to the new outlook—after 211 B.C.—particularly among young people, is that of all traditionally-minded Romans (Livy, 34, 4). In later periods, too, Romans, conscious of their city's mission, dissociated themselves from artistic activity, extending to it a benevolent tolerance but not taking it really seriously. There is no disputing Virgil's words:

> Let others better mold the running mass
> Of metals, and inform the breathing brass,
> And soften into flesh a marble face . . .
> But, Rome, 'tis thine alone, with awful sway,
> To rule mankind, and make the world obey,
> Disposing peace and war by thy own majestic way;
> To tame the proud, the fetter'd slave to free;
> These are imperial arts, and worthy thee.
>
> *(Aeneid*, VI, 847f., tr. John Dryden, Harvard Classics,
> ed. Charles W. Eliot, New York, 1909, p. 240.)

To such an extent was the world of politics divorced from that of art, even in the reign of Augustus; indeed, one can readily believe that ancient Rome was embellished only with bloodstained weapons looted from the foe; it seems that the question as to what works of art there were in such a city was meaningless. It is no use objecting that every people had produced art of some kind, and that the Romans can be no exception; for, if the existence of pictorial art is certainly not a matter of course, then it is undeniable that the Romans had no art of their own. All efforts to prove the contrary have inevitably failed. There is no reason for this fact to be suppressed out of respect for the magnificent achievements of the Roman people, nor does it mean that a regrettable shortcoming has been discovered, and that a dark shadow has been cast over the glorious image of ancient Rome; for it was not lack of artistic talent that prevented art from being born but the Roman concept of virtue, according to which an artist's occupation was incompatible with the ideal of a Roman citizen. Without hesitation one may agree with Cicero on this point: "If Fabius—a man of respectable lineage—had been at all regarded among us [instead of being mocked and called 'Pictor,' a name which remained in the family for centuries], the Romans too would have their artists like Polycletus [Polygnotus?] and Parrhasius" (Cicero, *Tusculanae Disputationes*, I, 2, 4). Thus the existence of a specifically Roman art is certainly not to be reckoned upon; even after 211 B.C. there was no fundamental change in this respect. For it was Greek art that found its way to Rome, the ancient "classical" art of past centuries, in the form of loot captured by victorious generals. There was also the new contemporary art of the Greek artists who now worked for and in Rome and were held in high esteem there, although less so than the *antiqui*, whose works were regarded as simply unsurpassable.

The flood of art that poured into Rome made the second century B.C. a period of upheaval and change, both in the external appearance of the city and in the Roman way of thinking. Pictorial art acquired a different role in people's lives; it gained higher prestige because, like Greek philosophy, it was associated with the high civilization to which Rome had now fallen heir. This was an unintended consequence of the Roman triumphs, so powerful that the victors felt that they had been defeated by their victims: "Greece, the captive, made her savage victor captive, and brought the arts into rustic Latium" (Horace, *Epist.*, II, 1, 156, tr. H. Rushton Fairclough, London–New York, 1926, p. 409).

Proud of their increasing ownership of property they had not earned, yet still mistrustful of it, the Romans began to romanticize their past. Now it was "rustic Latium," and "the wild, warlike race of Romulus." It was a band of stern, vigorous men which had directed the course of fortune in those ancient troubled times, when all the people's energy had been enlisted in the struggle against the Latins, Sabines, Volsci and Hernici, the Gauls (who had conquered the city), the mighty Etruscans, the battle-hardened Samnites, and Pyrrhus and the Carthaginians on land and at sea, and when the utmost exertion of the people had often done no more than ensure its own survival. Looking back from the present climax of achievement, and comparing its pretentious luxury with the simple puritanical virtues of the ancient citizens and peasants—the men who had laid the foundation of Rome's grandeur—the past now seemed as enviable as the life of a penniless shepherd who, for all his poverty, was nevertheless happy.

Deliberately turning away from the superficial splendor of their own age, from the magnificence of the princely courts, Greek Bucolic poets discovered the charms of nature and the natural life. The Romans, for their part, now had good reason to look back to a lost paradise. The founders of the city, Romulus and Remus, had been suckled by a she-wolf; exposed to die, they had been found by some shepherds and lived with them among their flocks. The city itself was the home of simple, brave, and puritanical men. "Religion was frugal and its rites spare, and there were no Capitols vying with the sky, but the altars were built casually of turf, the fumes rose sparsely from them, and the vessels were of Samian ware" (Tertullian, *Apol.*, 25). In this way we too have gained the fixed idea of ancient Rome as a city of wretched clay huts and narrow winding streets with herds of cattle being driven through crowds of carts and men on foot, a town of peasants and herdsmen who labored hard and fought valiantly—all this at a time when in Athens the Acropolis was being crowned by the Parthenon and Phidias was forging huge statues of the gods in gold and ivory. Indeed, for another two centuries, so it was asserted, Rome kept aloof from all Greek cultural influences, and it was not until a hundred years after Alexander the Great that the Greek Muse could find a foothold there.

In support of this picture of the period before 211 B.C. as one devoid of art, indeed inimical to it, which the ancient authors thought sound and worthy of emulation, they forbore to mention many facts that contradicted it. We know of these facts from incidental remarks; for example, Cato's defense of "the ancient clay temple decoration" from ridicule by young people who took Greek art as their yardstick. Thus already before 211 B.C. there existed pots, idols, and gable ends of clay (*antefixia fictilia*), i.e., works of art, even though of poor material. In part these hints to the contrary stem from an ancient tradition, opposed to that described above, which sought to compensate for any sense of an inferiority complex which might have arisen among the Romans. It stressed the fact that the Romans of old had long been familiar with works of art, and that painting and clay sculpture could boast of a very ancient tradition in Italy. Pliny's *Natural History* yields vital information in this respect, but of the utmost importance in this discussion are the interesting data in Livy's *History,* which never fails to mention in the accounts of Rome's military triumphs the booty that was taken. From this source we learn that not only cattle fell into the Romans' hands but also works of art, of which some were handed over as tokens of political subjugation, and others were associated with miraculous happenings.

Thus the nonartistic period of Roman history must be sought still further back, in the more distant past. This corresponds to another tradition, represented for example by Varro, according to which there were no statues in Rome during the first hundred and seventy years after the foundation of the city (Augustine, *De Civ. Dei*, IV, 31, etc.). This would mean that artistic activity began in the early sixth century B.C. This remark would therefore confirm the assumption that art did exist in ancient Rome, as well as Cicero's opinion that the ideas of those philosophers who lived and worked in Lower Italy, almost within the sight of his ancestors, at the time when Lucius Brutus freed the city from royal rule, probably penetrated as far as Rome *(Tusc.*, IV, 1).

To the north of Rome lay the mighty kingdom of the Etruscans, a less warlike but highly artistic people, while in the south were the flourishing cities of the Greek colonists. We may well ask, with Cicero, whether it was possible that both the art flourishing in the wealthy Greek colonies, so devoted to the refined pleasures of life, playing its part in the enrichment of life, the veneration of the dead, and the cults of the gods and heroes, and the art of the Etruscans, which stood in relation to Greek art in much the same special way as Roman art itself was later to stand, remained entirely without effect on Rome.

It is appropriate to attempt to connect the consideration of Etruscan and Lower Italian art with the search for traces of art in ancient Rome, because art in Italy had one source—Greek art—though the Etruscans, the Greeks of Lower Italy, and the Romans made greatly differing use of it.

National boundaries should not be drawn too sharply for this time; we are dealing not with nations in the literal sense but with groups of peoples who shared common political goals or a common culture rather than a common origin. Only in this way is it possible to understand the Etruscans, whose emergence from primeval darkness would seem so mysterious if one thought of them as a great homogeneous people, and whose eventual total disappearance would seem equally astonishing. They entered history as a political group comprising various indigenous and immigrant elements, and referred to themselves as "Rasena." "At first one became 'an Etruscan' not so much by one's descent as by one's own volition. The Falisci and Camerti remained Umbrians, as they had been from the start. But by political volition (no matter whether this was exercised through coercion or genuine free choice) they also became Etruscans" (Altheim). Regarded in this light, even the Romans were once Etruscans, in the period when they were ruled by the Tarquinian kings. But Roman conquest brought an end, not only to the Etruscan federation, but also to the very idea of an Etruscan people, and soon even the ancient language that had united the various elements in the federation passed into oblivion.

Nor was one necessarily "a Roman" by birth, particularly in earlier times. Fugitives from Troy or their descendants founded the city, but the people of the surrounding area were invited to settle there, and Rome came into being as an association of those who lived on its seven hills—thus ran the legend. Already at an early date it was a worthy ambition for a man to become a *civis Romanus*. Citizenship was conferred by a particular legal act, by adopting a Roman name, and by accepting the moral demands this implied. It was far from sufficient just to be a subject of Rome, to have fallen in one way or another under Roman rule. Not until the reign of Caracalla were all people in the Roman Empire made Roman citizens (A.D. 212).

The inhabitants of Magna Graecia, whether Greek settlers or natives, formed ethnically diverse groups mixed up together. Chalcidians, Phocaeans, Eretrians, Messenians, Ionians, Thessalians, Megarians, Troezenians, Achaeans, and Spartans sent out colonists who settled on the coasts of lands inhabited by Sicani, Siculi, Ausones, Aurunci, Chonaeans, Bruttians, Elymians, and Lucanians. The best known of these tribes

9

are the Samnites, who comprised four groups: Caudini, Hirpini, Pentri, and Frentani (Livy, VII, 29); they spoke Oscan, as did the Bruttians. A unifying factor here in Lower Italy was the Greek culture common to all groups of colonists, which the native peoples were able to absorb.

In addition to this, individual travelers, bands of warriors, merchants journeying by sea or by land, and temporary or lasting conquests forged contacts between the different parts of the country. How weak tribal bonds were and how much freedom of mobility there was can be seen from the fact that entire groups changed their tribal allegiance; there is also ample evidence of the custom of changing one's personal name. In the end, the successes achieved by the Roman armies as they conquered one part of Italy after another turned the old political boundaries into purely geographical ones.

With artists, too, tribal origin was of little account. They were not bound to any particular locality but moved from place to place wherever work was to be found. This was probably even more important in Italy than it was in Greece, for in any case less attention was paid here to tradition. The native Italic artistic tradition was no doubt often modified by immigrant Greek artists who came in search of better opportunities, especially when conditions in their homeland no longer suited them or they were obliged to flee after some political upheaval. There were ample reasons for them to emigrate: the fall of the tyrants, the Persian Wars or the Peloponnesian War, the civil strife of the fourth century, or the Macedonian conquest.

Thus ancient Italy may be seen as a geographically compact area reacting to the creative impulses flowing from the Greek motherland: a unity born out of the Etruscan, Magna Graecian, and Roman worlds.

The political history of Italy suggests that the relationship between these three areas—Etruria, Rome, and Magna Graecia—was continually changing. In the cultural field, too, there would have been hostility, closer and weaker ties, isolation and open-mindedness, activity and lethargy. For the first period, when Rome was still small and uninfluential, while the Etruscan realm in the north and the Greek cities in the south already boasted a flourishing cultural life, it would be possible to consider the three areas separately on the grounds that they were relatively isolated from each other, but even then many common features were already evident.

In the second period, when all Italy fell under Roman rule, Rome must be seen as the metropolis, Etruria and Lower Italy as provinces. Yet Italy as a whole formed virtually a unit from the artistic point of view, thus making it all the easier to draw conclusions from the rest of the country about the state of art in Rome.

In the third period, when Rome extended her power beyond the borders of Italy to Greece and the East, this unity was broken and Greek art proper entered the picture as a new element. It gave Rome an artistic preponderance over the rest of Italy, which was now of interest only as a mirror of artistic life in the capital; Etruria and Lower Italy, which had prepared the way for Greek artistic influence, were reduced to the rank of unimportant provinces. This decisive phase, to which the first two periods are but preliminaries, is the age of the Roman civil wars, of the Gracchi, of the Cimbric and Teutonic invasion, of Marius and Sulla, of Pompey and Caesar. The disturbed conditions which ensued were ill suited to the intellectual ferment unleashed everywhere once Rome had entered upon the heritage of Greek art. It was often necessary for political reasons to conceal one's respect and sympathy for Greek culture and art, since Roman custom still demanded that one ignore or despise everything alien; the very nudity, which played such a great role in Greek art, more than anything else aroused anger and invited rejection. It took some time before this objection could be overcome and a freer spirit held sway.

To be sure, art lovers in their enthusiasm sometimes did not shrink from crime. Verres abused his position in Sicily to rob the island of numerous works of art, and the governors in the East often showed no greater restraint. Others sought to build up their collections by purchases, paying enormous sums for Greek works both ancient and contemporary. Connoisseurs prized designs, models, and sketches by Greek masters, and art patrons as well as collectors made their appearance.

Interest in art was promoted by works on aesthetic theory. Thus Pasiteles wrote five books on art, some of which served Pliny as a source. Knowledge of history and the theory of art, as well as the lives and personalities of artists themselves, became more and more widespread. Arcesilaus, Apollonius, Tauriscus, Pasiteles, Cleomenes, and others achieved considerable fame and were in close contact with the great men of their day. They sought to imitate Greek works of the "classical" era, but at the same time stood in the tradition of late Greek art. Its forms, reminiscent of Baroque and Rococo, were held in esteem along with classicist ones, and no real compromise was ever effected between them. This became possible only when Augustus conferred the *Pax Romana* upon the world.

FROM AUGUSTUS TO CONSTANTINE

The Roman Empire up to the reign of Constantine was impressively rich in artistic production. Mighty buildings in Rome and the provinces, portraits of the emperors, historical reliefs and those on sarcophagi, altars, candelabra, fountains, and ornamental sculpture, not to mention numerous copies in marble of Greek bronze statues—all these suggest the existence of large workshops. Statues in precious metals and bronze, sometimes of vast dimensions, panel and wall paintings, mosaics, fine metalwork, and engraved gems also contributed not only to the decoration of public buildings and squares, and the houses and gardens of the rich, but bestowed the sheen of high civilization upon all aspects of life.

Appreciation of the ancient Greek works that were to be seen in public places and temples stimulated a desire to possess copies of them, if not the actual originals. Thus copies were made of pictures by Apelles and statues by Polycletus. The technical accomplishments of original masterpieces were carried over into copies in paint or mosaic, just as statues were copied in bronze and marble, or in dark stone imitating the patina of the original. The copies were not always true in every detail: they might alter the content or change the form for decorative purposes. The boundary between such independent reworking and fresh creative activity in the classicist spirit is a fluid one. Statuettes, coins, gems, sarcophagi, and silver and clay vessels perpetuate the classical repertoire of motifs without necessarily following them in every particular. It must be considered an especially fortunate circumstance that the rich possibilities of Greek art coincided with such a tremendous market for works of art: for not only did private persons want to enrich their lives in this way, but the characteristic Roman awareness of history demanded that the memory of great deeds be perpetuated for future generations through being carved in stone or cast in metal. Pictures representing the achievements of victorious heroes, triumphal arches crowned by the imperial quadriga, statues of the ruler erected throughout the Empire, imperial portraits on coins passed from hand to hand, richly ornamented public buildings and squares—all these were instruments of policy as well as part of Roman life. Art was the mouthpiece through which the emperor spoke to his people. For this reason "historical" pictures are not always simply accounts of certain historical events. The figure of the emperor is given special emphasis. He is treated as a superhuman being along with gods and allegorical figures.

The deification of an emperor had long been a feature of Greek art; the idea stemmed from Alexander and his successors. From the fifth century B.C. onward allegorical art served as a means of representing acts which portraiture had hitherto shunned, thereby filling a gap that had made art inferior to literature as a medium of expression. Henceforth such abstractions as *Roma, Virtus, Honos, Spes, Liberalitas,* or other ancient concepts could be personified, and new symbols were created for such typical Roman notions as *Senatus* or *Populus Romanus*.

Allegorical art also served to convey the alien Roman atmosphere in which the Greek artists lived and worked, and to which they soon adjusted themselves as their fellows had done earlier and elsewhere. For this reason Roman art of the Imperial period may unhesitatingly be described as Roman, for Roman ways of thought impregnated the Greek forms, not only through the outlook of the Roman patrons of art, but also through the outlook of Greek artists who themselves doubtless came to feel part of this Roman world. Yet in discussing "Roman" art, one must remember that the old Roman indifference to art remained, and that what distinguishes Imperial Roman art from the older Greek art is not that it is the Roman artistic talent as such which is being expressed, but simply that it was here that Greek art found new opportunities for self-expression—in the construction of splendid public squares, theaters, aqueducts, and palaces.

The Greek art of Imperial Rome was the final chapter in the history of the process whereby the influence of ancient Hellas spread throughout the Roman world. The course of Greek art was no longer in the direction of further spontaneous development: forces outside it, through the roles allotted to it according to the political climate at any given time, shaped and defined it down the centuries.

The reign of Augustus (27 B.C.–A.D.14) is of decisive significance for the entire Imperial period, in the artistic as well as in the political field. He gave Greek art and culture a firm place in Roman life; he sought also to adapt Greek art to Roman conditions by selecting from it what was felt to be appropriate. There was no place then for the unrestrained "baroque" works of the late Imperial period: fifth-century art with its simplicity and spirituality seemed to befit the reinvigorated Roman body politic better. On the other hand, early Italic art, felt to be characteristically "Roman," was taken as the foundation for what was customarily called "Augustan art," which was to set the course for later centuries.

This blend of old "classical" Greek art, Italic–late Greek art, and Augustan art, soon to be prized as a model, varied according to the taste of the reigning emperor, now one, now another component of the Augustan precedents being allowed to predominate, not even the baroque trend being permanently excluded.

Thus classicist and baroque periods alternate in Roman art. It is unmistakable that interest in the representation of external aspects dwindled through the convenient use of the seemingly inexhaustible creative heritage of the old art, and that this led to the employment of coarser means for the realization of pictorial ideas. In this gradual change one may detect a progressive line of development interrupted by periods of "renaissance." So far as content is concerned, Roman art became ever more politicized: as ideas of government changed and the principate of Augustus gradually gave way to unlimited absolutism, there was a corresponding shift of emphasis to purely pictorial modes of representation which had above all to be comprehensible. The aesthetic aspects of art, which the Romans had first come to appreciate in 211 B.C., thus lost much of their significance, and artists were in the last resort employed in satisfying current requirements for images, as in ancient times. Hence the astonishing similarity between many ancient Italic works and those of late Antiquity should not really surprise us.

The incorporation of Greece into the Roman Empire had kindled and nurtured the blossoming of Roman art, but at the same time had brought about the end of it as a source of inspiration for art in Italy. The stagnation resulting from the devastation of Greece was for a long time concealed from view by the magnificent achievements of the Greek artists who created the art of Rome; but eventually it becomes all too obvious that the thrusting energy behind Greek art had given out. The sense of beauty essential to the vitality of art reemerged in Europe only when "classical art" was rediscovered. The enthusiasm for Antiquity, which was of decisive importance for Renaissance art, could well have been like that which Marcellus inspired in the citizens of Rome through the exhibition of the Greek works of art he had captured in Syracuse. The spark that he kindled then ensured that Greek art would survive not only the political catastrophes which struck Greece, but also, through its cultivation in the Roman Empire, that it would have far-reaching influences on European culture in subsequent ages.

THE ORIGINS: EIGHTH CENTURY B.C.

Already in remote prehistoric times the influence of Greek sculpture and art was making itself felt in Italy. Greek legends tell of heroes who undertook voyages to the land in the West, and the finds of Mycenaean pottery in Sicily and Lower Italy confirm that early on there were fairly close links between the Italian peninsula and Greece. In the eighth century B.C., when the Greek colonists settled in large numbers along the coasts of Lower Italy and Sicily, probably they often came upon small Greek settlements and trading posts in these regions. Such cities as Crotona, Tarentum, Rhegium, Cyme, Pithecusa, and Sybaris in Lower Italy, and Naxos, Syracuse, Leontini, Catania, and Megara in Sicily, were founded during the eighth century, and

Greek culture also began to penetrate into the hinterland. It was at this time that Rome was founded (753 B.C.) and that native Umbrian tribes and immigrants from various parts of the Mediterranean formed a confederation in Etruria of wide-reaching power.

In this post-Mycenaean age, i.e., after the fall of Troy and the Mycenaean citadels in Greece (events which affected political conditions in Italy and which were mentioned in the legends of the founding of Rome and various Etruscan cities) art is Geometric in character, as it was at this time in Greece also. The ornamentation of the Villanovan culture, which succeeded the earlier Bronze Age cultures in about 900 B.C., undoubtedly shows Greek influence and changed the decoration then in use in a characteristic but quite uniform way.

Lid of an urn. Brown clay, height 11″. Eighth century B.C. From Vulci. Museo Nazionale di Villa Giulia, Rome

13

Figurative vessel. Clay, height 7″. Second half of eighth century B.C. From Bologna (Benacci tomb 525). Museo Civico, Bologna

The technique and decoration of the lid of a thick-walled, biconical urn (page 13) mark it out as characteristic of Villanovan art. Its shape resembles that of a helmet and also a house. The incised decoration has distinctive square panels with swastikas which look like parts of an intricate meander band.

This pipe-shaped vessel *(askos)* terminates in front in a bull's head and behind in a kind of funnel. The equestrian figure in between, shown wearing a helmet and carrying a shield, is worked in the round. Impressed and incised ornament extends over almost the entire surface of the vessel, the various bands of circles and hatching being adapted to its shape. Others, similar, likewise testify to the lively imagination behind these ancient indigenous artists' attempts at figurative representation.

Warrior. Bronze statuette, height 6¼″. Eighth century B.C. From Reggio, Emilia. Museo Civico, Bologna

The body of this warrior is only roughly indicated, whereas the head is quite finely modeled. The high-ridged helmet is of the common Villanovan type; it is also worn by the horseman on the Benacci *askos* (opposite page).

Shield. Bronze, diameter 25⅝″. Eighth century B.C. From Bisenzio (on Lake Bolsena). Museo Nazionale di Villa Giulia, Rome

This repoussé shield of sheet bronze is decorated with a pattern of concentric rings. The five attachments suspended inside probably served to make a noise. Remains of similar shields have been found in Rome and even in Olympia, whither this Italic shield must have found its way as a votive offering. In contrast to the usual Greek round shield this one has a handle in the middle, and is thus of the targe type.

Pyxis. Bronze, height 2⅝″, diameter 6¼″. Eighth century B.C. From a woman's tomb on the Esquiline, Rome. Antiquarium Comunale, Rome

This *pyxis,* an early forerunner of the cylindrical box (see page 116), was lined with wood on the inside. It is decorated with simple designs that recall those of the shield. On the lid and base are two triangular pro- —jections, to one of which the remains of a chain are affixed.

This biconical vessel has an ornament of rings containing dots and circles. The lid has a tall three-pronged superstructure, crowned by three figures; two of them are identifiable as warriors by the shield or sword they carry. The lid is apparently the helmet of the warrior whose ashes were deposited in the urn.

Urn. Bronze, height 29¼". Late eighth century B.C. Badisches Landesmuseum, Karlsruhe

Cup. Clay with dark-brown paint, height 5″. Eighth century B.C. From a tomb on the Esquiline, Rome. Antiquarium Comunale, Rome

This pot-bellied, single-handled cup is decorated round its widest part with a frieze of concentric circles drawn with the aid of compasses. This Roman vessel exemplifies particularly clearly the influence of Greek Geometric art. Remains of imported Greek vessels of this kind, one of which could have served as a prototype, have been discovered. They are the first direct evidence of cultural contacts between early Rome and Greece. Similar attempts to emulate the technique of Greek models were also made in Etruria, where, however, local pottery with incised Geometric motifs predominates (see page 13).

The strong oriental influence in Greek Geometric art is also dominant in seventh-century Etruria. At this time numerous objects of gold, silver, and bronze from the East reached Etruria and the environs of Rome. This oriental splendor soon led to imitations by native artists who often stubbornly adhered, however, to certain principles of Villanovan art.

The consolidation of Greek influence in Lower Italy, where more colonies were founded, probably prevented Etruscan art from becoming thoroughly orientalized and caused it to have a predominance of Greek elements. The fact that Proto-Corinthian vases were introduced and copied testifies to the close relations maintained with Greece, as does Pausanias' information (V, 12, 5) that Arimnestus, king of the Etruscans, dedicated to Zeus a throne in the temple at Olympia. The ancient authorities also record that at this time Greek artists came to Italy from Corinth.

Proto-Corinthian vessels also enjoyed high esteem in Rome, which according to later tradition was ruled by the kings Numa Pompilius, Tullus Hostilius, Ancus Marcius, and Tarquinius Priscus. Magna Graecia of itself developed an indigenous art which was closely akin to that of mainland Greece and manifested clearly the link with "Daidalic" art. Pottery, such as that of Cyme, appeared, a vigorous offshoot of the Proto-Corinthian prototypes; it too was exported to Etruria.

Warrior. Bronze, height 7". Early seventh century B.C. Supposedly discovered northeast of Rome. G. Ortiz Collection

This statuette still follows entirely the rectangular principles of composition of Geometric art. As in the case of the Bologna statuette (see page 15), the torso is less elaborately modeled than the face, which stands out masklike from beneath the helmet (see page 44), indicated only by the high plume. The warrior is wearing a strange garment resembling a swimsuit; his shield and lance are missing.

Fragments of about ten male and female statues were found in this princely tomb. It is not certain whether this head belongs to the torso. The spectacular decoration of the tomb throws light on the status of Etruscan rulers, which was comparable to that of the Greek tyrants. The artist, who gave elaborate attention to such details as the antithetical sphinxes on the metal belt, probably made use of oriental models.

Head and Torso (fragments). Limestone; life-size: height of head 11″, height of torso 25¼″. Mid-seventh century B.C. From the Pietrera Tomb at Vetulonia. Museo Archeologico Nazionale, Florence

Head. Light-red clay, 6¼ x 7½″. Mid-seventh century B.C. From an antefix found at Tarentum. Museo Civico, Trieste

With its wedge-shaped face framed by locks of hair, this head, jutting out from an *antefix* (ornament to conceal the ends of joint tiles of a roof), is reminiscent of Cretan and Corinthian works, as well as the Bologna head (see opposite) and the bronze warrior (see page 20).

Head of a Bearded Man. Dark sandstone, 10⅞ x 4¾″. Seventh century B.C. From Bologna. Museo Civico, Bologna ▶

This life-size head was part of the ornament on a tomb (statue or hermaean *cippus*). It is the only evidence we have for statuary in this area, apart from a single late sixth-century marble head. It might have been modeled upon a Magna-Graecian work (see above).

Caldron on tall stand. Bronze, height 70⅞". Early seventh century B.C. From the Tomba Bernardini ("Bernardini Tomb"), Praeneste (Palestrina). Museo Nazionale di Villa Giulia, Rome

This caldron and stand are products of oriental bronze workshops (Urartu) and found their way to central Italy as merchandise. The tomb contained other lavish gifts of gold, silver, ivory, and bronze, many of them likewise from the East. This splendid princely sepulcher near Rome, and another one similar to it, escaped the grave robbers because the ceiling caved in at an early date; consequently the whole of the contents is in a good state of preservation.

The caldron is decorated with griffin heads and attachments fashioned like sirens and the stand with two pairs of winged fabulous beasts.

Shield handle. Bronze, plated with silver, height 4⅞". Early seventh century B.C. From the Tomba Bernardini ("Bernardini Tomb"), Praeneste (Palestrina). Museo Nazionale di Villa Giulia, Rome

The outer side of this handle is embellished with antithetical groups of figures, as in a coat of arms: horses rear up opposite one another, deities tame fabulous monsters, or men slay a lion. The style of this relief is reminiscent of oriental work. The inner side of the handle has plaited bands and animal friezes, which make it an interesting example of the fusion of native Geometric art with that of the Orient.

◄ The youth is rendered in the same way as early Greek *kouroi* (sculptured figures of Greek youths or athletes), and the woman as in Greek works of the seventh century B.C. In spite of the delicate manner of execution variations from the Greek ideal are noticeable, especially in the proportions of the youth. It remains doubtful whether these statuettes were imported or were carved in Rome by a Greek or native master.

Together with two similar female statuettes (now in London) and others of which only fragments have survived, this seated man was part of the furnishings of a tomb and, like the other pieces, probably represented a deceased member of the family. He is wearing a light-brown undergarment and a cloak in a darker color; the unclothed parts are yellowish. The cloak is fastened at the right shoulder by an intricate fibula. With the bold modeling of the body it is surprising to find such a delicate rendering of the face recalling the best Greek works of the period.

◄ Two figurines. Ivory, height of the male statuette $1^5/8''$, of the female one $1^3/4''$. Late seventh century B.C. From the Forum Romanum (near the Lapis Niger), Rome. Antiquario Forense, Rome

Man Sitting. Clay, height $18^1/2''$. Early or mid-seventh century B.C. From Caere (Cerveteri) or Montalto di Castro. Palazzo dei Conservatori, Rome

This unusually large and lavishly decorated fibula comes with certainty from a tomb furnished as splendidly as the tombs at Praeneste (Palestrina), or the Regolini-Galassi tomb at Caere (Cerveteri) in which a comparable fibula has been found. Both fibulas have granulation and filigree ornament, but on the one from Vulci the near-oval disk is incised. In the ornamental area we can make out a combat scene, two lions, and several birds in flight, and in the center a cross which, like the drawings, is in the traditional Villanovan style. The small animals on the longitudinal axis look oriental. The disk and the lower part of the fibula are executed in different techniques; they were at any rate joined together in the seventh century, although originally they may have been separate.

Cruciform object. Bronze, height of human figures 3¹/₂″, overall length 8⁵/₈″. Seventh century B.C. From the Tomba Bernardini ("Bernardini Tomb"), Palestrina. Museo Nazionale di Villa Giulia, Rome

◀ Fibula. Gold, height 7³/₄″. Seventh century B.C. From Vulci (Ponte Sodo). Antikensammlung, Munich

This and another very similar piece served as the decoration of a wooden implement. Affixed to it are statuettes of men wearing loincloths and protruding foliage garlands, and of imaginary animals, which show clearly the work of a native artist who succeeded in combining the Villanovan tradition with concepts introduced from the Orient.

Pyxis. Ivory, height $8^5/_8''$, diameter at top $6^1/_4''$ and $5^1/_2''$, at base $6^1/_4''$. End of seventh century B.C. From the Pania tumulus, Clusium (Chiusi). Museo Archeologico Nazionale, Florence

This pyxis, worked from a single piece of ivory, is decorated with four friezes separated by bands of palmettes. The two lower friezes are of animals, a centaur and a man on horseback being introduced in the upper of these two registers. The topmost register depicts Odysseus' flight from the cave of Polyphemus, and the second one a funeral procession with musicians, dancers, warriors, and wailing women. The style of this unique work betrays oriental influence, but the subject matter indicates a knowledge of Greek legends.

Two beakers. *Bucchero*, height 6¼″ and 5½″. Late seventh century B.C. From the Tomba dei Leoni Dipinti ("Tomb of the Painted Lions"), Caere (Cerveteri). Museo Nazionale di Villa Giulia, Rome

The shape of these clay vessels, with their loop handles on the rim, is unusual and suggestive of a bucket. The potter may have copied a metal vessel, or alternatively one of ivory. In any case these beakers are akin to the ivory pyxis from Clusium (opposite) in their division into registers, in the alternation between ornamental friezes and those with figures, and even in certain matters of detail, such as the man with a sword in one of the animal friezes, showing that a mythological element has crept in. Lions in the same style were painted upon the wall of the tomb in which these beakers were found.

Bucchero pottery, consisting of black clay either decorated with reliefs or with the surface left smooth, was to be characteristic of Etruria for a long time to come.

This egg-shaped vessel, resting
upon a tall curved base and with
a neck of similar shape, is for the
greater part covered with reliefs;
there are palmette ornaments on
the neck and base as well as upon
the belly of the vessel, where they
are enclosed within animal friezes.
The handle, of which the upper
part is flat and the lower part
curved, has on top three horse
protomai (head and neck of an
animal); on top of the lid is a
projecting floral design. This vessel is a blend of native, oriental,
and Greek elements.

This pyxis rests on three tall feet suggestive of an animal's legs. It has an incised palmette design, and on the
lid three birds arbitrarily modeled in a Geometric manner—as one also finds on Etruscan painted pottery.
The knob on the lid is ornamented with protruding bosses and circles. This and similar vessels from Rome exhibit a peculiar fusion of Latin and Etruscan elements. The technique employed in the incising is Italic; the
patterns are based on Greek models; the shape of the vessel is probably an imitation of one in metal.

The form of government in Italy was monarchy, i. e., a *tyrannis,* and in this respect was no different from that of Greece. Conditions in Etruria may be deduced only from what is known of Rome, which was ruled by Servius Tullius, originally known as Macstrna, and Tarquinius Superbus, and from what is known of Sicily under such tyrants as Phalaris of Acragas. The Etruscan confederation of city-states extended its power from the Po valley to Campania, so attaining its maximum extent, and maintained very different relations with the Greeks and the Carthaginians. Its art is distinguished by an unsophisticated serenity and splendor that clearly suited the aristocratic way of life in the ruling cities.

A large part of all the finds in Magna Graecia and Etruria stems from this century. For later generations the term "Tuscan art" was synonymous with archaic art as such. Receptivity toward alien influences, characteristic of the *tyrannis,* is evident in Etruria from the fact that taste fluctuated in favor of Corinthian, Ionian, and finally Attic art, and that a large number of Corinthian and Attic vases was imported.

Massive temples enhanced the splendor of the cities and the fame of those who built them. In Rome under the Tarquinian rulers the Temple of Jupiter was erected on the Capitoline Hill, and to embellish it the Etruscan artist Vulca was summoned to Rome from Veii. Corinthian, Laconian, and Attic pottery also found its way to Rome, where besides Latin both Etruscan and Greek were understood.

Temple at Paestum. Solid porous limestone, formerly covered with stucco, 80′ 5″ × 178′. c. mid-sixth century B.C.

This temple in the south of the area of temples at Paestum was formerly called "the Basilica" but is today known as the temple of Hera. It is the earliest of the three temples still standing, the most impressive reminder of the Greek colonies in southern Italy. The squat columns (nine in the facade and eighteen along the sides) taper markedly toward the top and are beautifully decorated in part below the capitals. The temple served the cults of two deities and for this reason was divided into two parts. Seven columns separate the two aisles of the cella, and a column in the exact center of the facade indicates through its position that the temple had two entrances.

◄ This vessel, in which Greek forms have been only slightly modified, is executed in the ancient Italic ceramic technique, but the whole surface is covered with ornament. The wavy bands, lingulate designs, triangles, and the ray pattern at the mouth all indicate Greek influence, whereas the frieze of rounded palmettes points to oriental prototypes. The tomb yielded another amphora of this kind, together with imported Greek Proto-Corinthian pottery.

Amphora. Red clay *(impasto)* with painting in white, height 18″. c. 600 B.C. From Caere (Cerveteri). Museo Nazionale di Villa Giulia, Rome

Mother-Goddess. Yellowish limestone with slight traces of paint, height 30³/₄″. First half of sixth century B.C. From the necropolis at Megara Hyblaea. Museo Nazionale, Syracuse

The goddess is depicted seated upon a throne, wrapped in a cloak and suckling two babies lying across her lap. The massive forms of her body, and indeed the whole feeling of the statue, are entirely non-Greek, indicating that native ideas are at work here. The numerous representations of the mother-goddess at Capua are later in date.

Standing Goddess. Gypsum, height 34⁵/₈″. c. 560 B.C. From the "Tomb of Isis" (Polledrara necropolis), Vulci. British ▶ Museum, London. Left: front view. Right: back view

This column-like figure gazes ahead sternly, her forearms stretched out horizontally before her. In her right hand she probably held a bowl and in her clenched left hand she grasped some thin object. She is wearing a girdled undergarment, the lower part of which is ornamented with a frieze of lotus palmettes, and a cloak with a ladder-like design on the hem. Her hair hangs down her back in thick queues and is carefully bound round at the end with a band. The Etruscan artist has taken over Greek forms with little alteration. Nothing is known about the significance of this figure, which was part of the tomb furnishing.

Centaur. Stone, height 30¹/₄″. c. 600 B.C. From Vulci. Museo Nazionale di Villa Giulia, Rome

This bearded horse-demon is depicted in wholly human guise, as was also common practice in early Greek art, except that here the horse's body grows from the middle of the human back. The centaur's hands are placed upon the thighs, locks of hair fall upon the low brow and the nape of the neck, and over the ears there are thick twisted skeins of hair.

This section of a frieze, which extends over the adjoining triglyph as well as the metope, depicts Heracles bearing off the captured Cercopes like a hunter carrying bagged hares; but despite their predicament these good-for-nothings, who wanted to rob Heracles while he was asleep, still manage to make some witty remarks about what they can see from this angle, so that finally Heracles lets them go free.

The Treasury was decorated all around with metopes illustrating various episodes in the legend in a crude style which nevertheless has an almost three-dimensional effect.

Heracles and the Cercopes. Metope from the Treasury in the Temple of Hera at Foce del Sele. Sandstone, $32^{3}/_{8} \times 53^{1}/_{8}''$. Second half of sixth century B.C. Museo Archeologico, Paestum

This tablet, which on top has an incised palmette band and a cyma rendered partially in the round, depicts Europa being abducted by Zeus in the guise of a bull. Together with three other metopes in relief (Sphinx; Apollo, Artemis, and Leto; and Heracles and the Bull), this decoration was part of the facade of a temple which was later (before 409 B.C.) demolished and reconstructed.

Europa Riding the Bull.
Metope from the earliest
temple at Selinus. Lime-
stone with traces of paint
(red in the background and
on the bull's eyes, black on
the pupil, and blue on the
bull's tail), height 33⅛".
Mid-sixth century B.C. Museo Archeologico Nazio-
nale, Palermo

Europa Riding the Bull.
Caeretan hydria. Clay with
glaze paint and pale body
color, height 17⅝". From
Caere (Cerveteri). Museo
Nazionale di Villa Giulia,
Rome

The category of Caeretan *hydriae* (water jars) is distinguished by the particular vitality of the representations and by the decorative quality of the ornament. It is regarded as undoubtedly Etruscan today, whereas it was formerly thought that these vases probably developed in the east of the Greek world. The strong in-fluence of Ionian art is unmistakable. On the far side of this hydria are two winged horses.

Youth. Bronze, height 9½". c. 500 B.C. From Corinaldo (Val di Cesano). Museo Archeologico, Ancona

This statuette portrays a young man with short hair curled over his brow and the nape of his neck, standing in an attitude of composure, like a Greek *kouros;* however, his fists are not clenched, and his hands rest outstretched upon his thighs. It is uncertain whether this is an imported Etruscan piece or whether it was worked according to Etruscan prototypes in the area where it was found, in Picenum.

This statue represents a young man of the *kouros* type and bears the incised inscription upon the right thigh: "To Sombrotidas, the son of Mandrocles, the physician ..." Since the statue can hardly portray a physician, it seems to have been dedicated by one of the physician's patients whose name was recorded in the continuation of the inscription upon the lower part of the leg, since lost. This statue is one of the most important archaic sculptures in Magna Graecia, hardly distinguishable from the *kouroi* of the homeland.

Statue for Sombrotidas. Marble, height 46⁷/₈″. Mid-sixth century B.C. From Megara Hyblaea. Museo Nazionale Archeologico, Syracuse

43

Warrior. Limestone with paint, height 86¼″. Mid-sixth century B.C. From Capestrano (Aquila province). Museo Nazionale di Antichità, Chieti

This statue, carved by a Picenian sculptor, represents a warrior in full armor (for the loincloth, cf. page 20). The insecure stance, the use of two supports featuring a fairly long inscription and incised lances, and last but not least the masklike face, show that the artist was not quite able to equal his Greek model; the latter, the *kouros,* is represented in a state of equipoise, without any supports. Most of the plume on the helmet has been restored since ancient times. Remains of other figures, including female ones, testify to the widespread activity of this provincial master.

Statuettes. Bronze, height 3″; 2½″. Sixth century B.C. From the Forum Romanum (near the Lapis Niger), Rome. Antiquario Forense, Rome

On either side of the man holding a crook in his hands, whose proportions and posture are evidence of strong affinities with the local art tradition, are male and female statuettes, found here and at other sites in Rome, which bear the distinct imprint of Greek art. The discovery in Rome of imported Greek pottery from various workshops testifies to the wide-ranging contacts which the city had, and which served as sources of inspiration to artists working there.

45

The eastern facade of this "central fortress temple" was decorated with metopes, of which the other ones surviving show Heracles' adventure with the Cercopes (see page 39) and two quadrigae viewed frontally. The slaying of Medusa by Perseus, attended by his protectress Athena, is of particular interest because it shows the birth of Pegasus upon the death of Medusa, which was rarely represented in this connection. Athena's head was added later.

Perseus Slaying Medusa. Metope on Temple C at Selinus. Limestone with traces of paint, 57⅞ × 43¾". c. 520 B.C. Museo Nazionale Archeologico, Palermo

Head. Clay with traces of black paint on the hair and eyebrows, height 3¹/₈″. Mid-sixth century. From the Forum Romanum (near the Lapis Niger, together with 26 and 45), Rome. Antiquario Forense, Rome

This small head originally represented a girl, but was later transformed into that of a man by the addition of a beard. Stylistically it recalls the metopes at Selinus (see page 46) and the symposiast at Tarentum (see page 57), thus pointing to Magna-Graecian influence.

Three Goddesses. Clay with glaze paint and white and red color, 39³/₄ × 22¹/₂″. c. 550 B.C. From Caere (Cerveteri). British Museum, London

Two of the women are holding ointment jars, while the third grasps her girdle, one end of which is wound round the lower part of her body.

Of five painted clay plaques from a sepulchral chamber at Caere, which came into the possession of the British Museum, two are decorated with a sphinx and the others with three human figures. They are caught in various attitudes of motion; below them is a row of tall planks, and above an intricate plaited design.

Woman's Head. Bronze, height 4³/4″. c. 550 B.C. From Castel San Mariano, near Perugia. Museo Archeologico, Perugia

This head and another one not so well preserved are in repoussé bronze delicately chased around the eyes and eyebrows. Kindred bronze reliefs, from the embellishment of a luxurious chariot (see overleaf), were found in the same area. They originated from the same workshop; owing to their high quality they were at first thought to be Greek.

Procession of Chariots. Clay with paint, 9½ x 23⅜". c. 530 B.C. From the Esquiline, Rome. Antiquarium Comunale, Rome

This plaque of a frieze from a chamber tomb on the Esquiline represents a succession of chariots—imaginary ones, as is evident from the fact that one pair of horses is winged. Some fragments of plaques made from the same mold have also been discovered on the Palatine, and others have been found at Velletri. From this it can be concluded that the subject was a man with Cerycaion (Hermes?) standing in front of the three-horse chariot.

The discovery at various places of reliefs from the same mold shows how little art was bound to a particular locality during this period.

◀ This luxurious chariot (for the shape, see above) is lavishly decorated with bronze reliefs. The largest of those on the front apparently depicts Hephaestus handing over to Achilles the weapons he has forged. The panel on the right-hand side of the chariot portrays a duel fought over someone's body, and on the left-hand side there is a chariot with winged horses shown running over a woman. At the points where these join the front panel, there is the figure of a naked youth. The lower part of the chariot is rounded off with smaller relief friezes featuring groups of animals in combat, a centaur, and a man fighting a lion. A similar chariot recently discovered at Ischia di Castro (Latium) is adorned with only the figures of the two youths.

Thetis and Achilles (?). Front of a chariot. Bronze, height 33⅜". c. 550 B.C. From Monteleone, near Spoleto. The Metropolitan Museum of Art, New York City

The horse stands out against a dark-brown ground; of his rider there remain only the plume of his helmet, his lance, and one foot. The tall plume encroaches upon a molding decorated with a pattern of arches. This relief was used to decorate a building. The style shows a very individual treatment of natural forms to produce an ornamental effect.

Man on Horseback. Clay with paint, 9¼ × 7⅞″. From the Forum Romanum (near the Lapis Niger), Rome. Antiquario Forense, Rome

Wall painting. c. 500 B.C. From the Tomba del Barone ("Tomb of the Baron"), Tarquinia

Opposite a woman with both hands raised majestically stands a man of noble appearance, holding a bowl and tenderly embracing a little flutist. To the left and to the right there is a youth on horseback. On one of the side walls of the sepulchral chamber a woman is portrayed framed by young men with horses; on the opposite wall the woman is missing. The paint is applied to a ground which, however, leaves the intermediate areas free. A striking feature is the lavish vegetation, which adds a cheering note to the earnest treatment of the scene.

Turan (Aphrodite). Marble, height of torso 22″, of entire statuette c. 35³/₈″. Mid-sixth century B.C. From the Necropole del Crocefisso del Tufo, Orvieto. Museo Orvieto

Goddesses were not portrayed naked in Greek art at this period; moreover, this marble statuette stood within a complex of tombs. These facts suggest that it must have represented a specifically Etruscan deity. A goddess, Venus Libitina, in part Aphrodite and in part goddess of death, was known in Central Italy and Rome. The marble for it must have been imported, since this is not found in Etruria; the artist may have been a Greek who settled in Orvieto and adapted himself to Etruscan conditions. Numerous gold accessories are now lost. The large parts of the legs missing have been filled out with plaster.

This goddess has sphinxes standing upon her shoulders and holds another sphinx as an attribute in her right hand. She is schematically rendered in accordance with the Greek *korai* (sculptured female representations). The Magna-Graecian style has been transformed by the individual treatment of the drapery, the proportioning, and other details. The combination of an Aphrodite-like goddess with the death symbol of the sphinx also suggests that this mirrorstand was produced near its place of discovery, since the concept of such a goddess, supreme over life and death, was native to Etruria and Rome (see opposite). The mirror and base are missing.

Goddess. Mirrorstand. Bronze, height 9¼". c. 510 B.C. From the environs of Rome. British Museum, London

Reclining Couple. Pair on the lid of a sarcophagus. Clay, height of sarcophagus 55$^1/_8$″, length 78$^3/_4$″. c. 510 B.C. From Caere (Cerveteri). Museo Nazionale di Villa Giulia, Rome

The custom of a man and a woman lying together upon the *clinium* (couch) at a banquet was contrary to Greek notions, but was generally practiced in Etruria. Thus a smallish chest containing ashes recently discovered at Caere shows a man and a woman reclining like this.. The tender relationship between the figures rules out any thought that the woman might be a hetaera (courtesan); she is the equal of her partner (see page 130). This group is a splendid example of Etruscan terra-cotta art for its techniques both of modeling and of firing.

The *symposiast* (banqueter) reposing upon his clinium holds a bowl in his right hand and a lyre in his left. This Greek youth is strongly reminiscent of the banquet scenes in Etruscan tombs (see page 87), similar examples of which also occur at Paestum; of the figures on the lids of Etruscan sarcophagi (see opposite); and of reliefs on cinerary urns (see over).

Recumbent Symposiast. Clay, height 8″. c. 530 B.C. From Tarentum. Museo Nazionale Archeologico, Taranto

Such urns for ashes, worked in local stone, are confined to Clusium. Depicted in characteristic low relief is a banqueting scene of a kind familiar from numerous Greek vases. It conveys the notion of the afterlife of the soul—as also expressed through banquets or dances (as on the reverse of this urn) in the paintings in the tombs. Recently a painting of a similar banqueting scene was found in a tomb at Paestum.

Banquet. Cinerary urn. Sandstone, 15 × 24³/₄″. End of sixth century. From Clusium. Museo Archeologico Nazionale, Florence

Girls Running. Metope from the Temple of Hera at Foce del Sele. Sandstone, 33½ × 28¼″. Museo Archeologico, Paestum

Of the six metopes in relief on this temple, five repeat the motif of two girls running, whereas the sixth portrays an *Amazonomachy* (Battle of the Amazons). As yet no acceptable explanation has been offered for these groups of girls, executed by various hands and based upon a model. Their late archaic excellence contrasts with the vigorous metopes of the earlier Treasury (see page 39).

Dancer. Supporting figure of an incense stand. Bronze, height 7⅛", of complete stand 14". c. 490 B.C. From Vulci. Badisches Landesmuseum, Karlsruhe

A naked youth is performing a lively dance upon a lavishly articulated socle, which itself rests upon a base decorated with small ducks and supported by three lions' legs. He is wearing soft leather shoes with flaps and has rings on his arms. Above his head rises a shaft, the lower part of which is ornamented in the manner of a *polos* (the high cylindrical headdress or crown of a deity) and with a garland of rays. Etruscan artists repeatedly demonstrated an astonishing skill in combining human figures with implements (see pages 91, 113). The artists of Lower Italy likewise felt free from the restraints which apparently bound Greek artists in this respect (see pages 120 f.).

This trough-shaped urn was a receptacle for the ashes of the dead, like the stone urns from Clusium (see page 58). The young man and horses on the sides of this urn were painted in a style reminiscent of these and of the murals in the tombs (see page 53).

Painted urn. Clay, 14¾ × 19½". c. 500 B.C. From Tarquinia. Museo Nazionale, Tarquinia

Seascape. Wall painting in the Tomba della Caccia e Pesca ("Tomb of Hunting and Fishing"), Tarquinia. c. 520 B.C.

All round the walls of the rear chamber of this tomb there runs a seascape. One sees fishermen casting out their nets, a man standing on a cliff snaring birds, and another jumping off a cliff. This painting is unique both in its size and in the variety of themes from nature treated so gaily, for which there are hardly any Greek prototypes. The motif of the man jumping off the cliff indeed occurs also in a tomb painting recently discovered at Paestum.

Heracles. Clay, height 29⁷/₈″. c. 520 B.C. From ▶
Rome (near Sant'Omobono). Antiquarium Comunale, Rome

This figure of Heracles trampling upon a hind
he has caught stood with other life-size terracotta statues above the ridgepole of a temple
at Veii. The torso from Rome was likewise
part of the decoration of a temple, of which
other parts have survived (see page 64).

Heracles. Clay with paint, height 63″. c. 500 B.C.
From Veii. Museo Nazionale di Villa Giulia, Rome

It is very likely that this head belongs to one of the statues ▶
which stood above the ridgepole of the temple (see above).
The head is modeled boldly and with a sureness of touch,
its lines expressing an evident joy in life. This is characteristic of Veiian art, which enjoyed great fame as is
attested by the fact that Vulca was summoned from Veii
to Rome. Ionic and Attic elements are at the root of its
very individual style, which blends robustness with a gay
vitality.

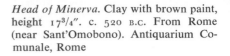

Head of Minerva. Clay with brown paint, height 17¾″. c. 520 B.C. From Rome (near Sant'Omobono). Antiquarium Comunale, Rome

◄ *Head*. Fragment. Clay with paint, height 7½″. c. 500 B.C. From Veii. Museo Nazionale di Villa Giulia, Rome

Head of Silenus. Clay with traces of paint, height 13³/₈″. c. 500 B.C. From an antefix on the Esquiline, Rome. Antiquarium Comunale, Rome

Several Roman temples, including that of Jupiter on the Capitol, had Silenus heads on their antefixes. The double-ended mustache and the beard with its horizontal wavy lines show a trend toward mannerism.

◄ The long hair flowing down the nape of the neck identifies this head as female and the helmet indicates Minerva. The shape of the helmet, with its tall plume, is common in Etruria. This Minerva figure together with others, of which the Heracles torso on page 62 is a survival, was probably part of the decoration of a temple.

The walls of this chamber tomb are decorated with pictures of wailing men and funeral performances in honor of the deceased. These depict runners, pugilists, men tugging on a rope, and two well-built wrestlers in the typical starting posture. Next to these sporting contests is the grisly group in which someone is being mauled by a dog held on a leash by a man in a mask. This connects the scene with the gladiatorial combats which originally took place also in honor of the deceased. The referee to the left of the wrestlers has erroneously been taken to be an augur, on account of his crook and the birds in flight; hence the tomb's name. The style of the paintings is close to that of the Caeretan hydriae (see page 41).

Wrestlers. c. 540 B.C. From the Tomba degli Auguri ("Tomb of the Augurs"), Tarquinia

This figure, seated upon a throne, is probably Persephone and may have been the cult image of a temple. In her right hand the goddess held a bowl, and in her left an attribute. The statue was at first thought to have been imported from Greece (Aegina), but it now seems certain that it was made in Tarentum. An archaic style is still evident in the treatment of detail, but despite the frontal pose one can sense the new currents introduced by Greek art. Old and new elements are blended with particular charm in this work from the Greek colonies.

Seated Goddess. Marble, height 59½". c. 480 B.C. From Tarentum. State Museums, Berlin

This head of a woman, wearing a polos-like diadem, and made from a mold of an original model, is stylistically akin to Ionic works but in its essentials corresponds to Attic *korai*. Large numbers of similar female heads, modeled only on the front, have been found in sacred precincts in Sicily.

This young man, whose subtle smile recalls the terra-cotta head from Syracuse (see page 69), has three rows of little curls across his brow; the torso can be reconstructed from the *kouros* torsos of the same area. His lively spirit is in conformity with the freer, less inhibited attitude toward their environment developed by people living in the Greek colonies.

Head of a Young Man. Marble, height 10⁷/₈″. c. 500 B.C. From Leontini (Lentini). Museo di Castello Ursino, Catania

This head, which with its triple row of curls recalls the young man from Leontini (see opposite), is probably of the goddess Diana, who was
worshiped on the banks of Lake Nemi. She is
depicted in a similar form on a coin dating from
the first century B.C. The expression seems to
convey a peculiarly Latin alertness (see pages
73–5).

Head of Diana Nemorensis. Fragment of a statue (the
eyes were formerly painted). Bronze, height 8¼". c. 500
B.C. From Aricia. Ny Carlsberg Glyptotek, Copenhagen

Head of a Deity. Marble, height 10¹/₄″. End of sixth century B.C. From Volterra. Museo Guranacci (from a private collection, on loan), Volterra

This head, larger than life-size, of a young man with wide-open eyes formerly inlaid in color, probably belonged to the figure of a god. His long hair, which falls down over his brow and his temples, is coiled at the back in a garland. In spite of the close affinities with Greek art as regards the material (see page 54) and the style, the posture and the unusually alert expression are markedly Etruscan.

This small head throws light upon the art of Rome toward the end of the period of the kings, when the Temple of Jupiter was built on the Capitol. It is reminiscent of Attic *korai,* except that the brow is lower. The painted eyelashes give the large eyes a particularly lively expression, and the plain coiffure emphasizes the simplicity of the maidenly ideal.

Girl's Head. Clay with details painted in black, height 5³/₄″. End of sixth century B.C. From an antefix on the Palatine, Rome. Antiquario Palatino, Rome

Tinia. Clay, height 9⁷⁄₈″. c. 500
B.C. From Satricum. Museo Nazionale di Villa Giulia, Rome

This dignified, severe head is
probably an image of Tinia,
the Italic form of Zeus; remains of a thunderbolt have
also been found. The eyes were
probably covered with a
brightly colored substance.
The slight indication of a
smile enlivens the austerity of
this deity. In contrast to
Etruscan clay statues from
Veii, the sculptures from Satricum show an individual Latin
style (see page 71).

Head of a Maiden (Juno?). Clay ▶
with yellow coating and brown
paint, height 3⁷⁄₈″, c. 500 B.C.
From Signia (Segni). Museo Nazionale di Villa Giulia, Rome

This vigorous little head is part of a votive gift to Juno, to whom a temple was dedicated on the acropolis at
Signia. It is surprising to find such fine miniature work in this part of the country, inhabited by the Volsci,
whom we know from Roman history only as savage warriors. The back of the head is covered by a veil.

The Temple of Athena at Paestum. Limestone, 50′ 1″ × 107′ 10″. End of sixth century B.C.

The northern temple in the sacred precinct at Paestum is known, from an inscription upon a shard, to have been dedicated to Athena. It deviates in many respects from the typical Greek temple. Thus at the foot of the pediment the horizontal cornice is missing and the coffering on the sloping cornices gives an impression of the eaves simply having been left to overlap the gable ends. The *pronaos* (space between the front wall of the cella and the front steps of a temple) of the Doric building contained six Ionic columns. Other details also show that here we have the development of a local style.

FIFTH CENTURY B.C.

The most decisive event in Roman history, the expulsion of the kings and the foundation of a republic, was dated by ancient authorities at 510 B.C., the same year as that which saw the fall of the tyrants in Athens. In Etruria, too, the monarchy was evidently weakening. Only in Magna Graecia did conditions remain unchanged: huge temples, votive offerings by Sicilian princes to Delphi, and the splendor of courts which could attract such poets as Pindar, Bacchylides, and Aeschylus, all indicate that under the rule of the tyrants the Greek colonies flourished. The victory over the Carthaginians near Himera in 480 B.C. provided the economic and political security that made this possible.

The radical breach with the archaic style which took place in Athens also had decisive consequences in Italy, in that the art styles of Etruria and Magna Graecia ceased to be autonomous and strongly individualistic variants of the Greek: in some parts the archaic style was continued, while in others new borrowings prevailed; in either case Greek art was the active, Italian the passive and receptive partner. This was true despite the activity in Magna Graecia of Pythagoras, one of the pioneers of the new style, and the fact that both in Etruria and in Magna Graecia the most delightful objects were still being produced in the archaic style or in a blend of this with the new style.

In Rome the breach with the Etruscans did not bring about any basic artistic reorientation; the links remained in being despite Rome's increased self-awareness and its marked rapprochement with the Greeks in the south. According to ancient sources in 493 B.C. two Greek artists (probably from Lower Italy), Damophilus and Gorgasus, decorated the Temple of Ceres in Rome with paintings and images modeled in clay. Up to this time art in Rome had been Etruscan; it was thenceforth Greek (Pliny, 35, 154). Of fifth-century marble originals discovered in Rome, most of them certainly the work of Magna-Graecian artists, some were probably made for the Roman market and were not booty. Other Roman temples besides that of Ceres may have provided an occasion for Greek artists to be summoned to Rome, as Etruscan artists had been under the monarchy, to supply the decoration and the cult image.

Thus prior to its seizure by the Gauls in 387 B.C. Rome may have presented a picture justifying Heraclides Ponticus' description of it (in Plutarch, *Cam.,* 22) as a "Greek city."

This unusually well-preserved temple is the work of an architect familiar with the Temple of Zeus at Olympia. The cella is divided into three aisles by two rows of superimposed columns. This temple produces its effect simply by its balanced proportions, for there is no sculptural ornamentation of any kind to divert the eye from the noble beauty of the monument.

Temple of Hera at Paestum. Shell lime covered with stucco 196′ 6″ x 79′ 9″. Shortly before the mid-fifth century B.C.

◀ Temple E at Selinus. Limestone covered with stucco, 222′ 2″ × 83′. Shortly before the mid-fifth century B.C.

The architecture of Temple E at Selinus shows clearly that the Temple of Zeus at Olympia served as prototype. In both cases only the metopes of the shorter sides are covered with reliefs: each of the six metopes shows a male and female figure face to face (see below and opposite). This temple is the last great monument to be built at Selinus and was probably destroyed when the Carthaginians sacked the city in 409 B.C.

Zeus and Hera. Metope from Temple E at Selinus. Limestone, formerly covered with stucco and paint; Hera's flesh in marble, height 67³/₄″. c. 460 B.C. Museo Archeologico Nazionale, Palermo

◀ The artist here dispensed with attributes and characterized Hera by her proud, majestic stance and Zeus by the grandeur of his gesture; he is holding the goddess by her wrists as she unveils herself before him. The divine nature of these two figures is expressed in their ennobled humanity and in the unusual rapture of their gaze, full of the intimacy of a man's and a woman's relationship.

The hunter Actaeon has been transformed into a stag, with the consequence that his own hounds attack him. The scene is here presented realistically: Actaeon is wearing over his shoulders the stag's skin, and with a gentle sign of her hand Artemis is setting the pack onto their master, for whom there is no salvation.

Artemis and Actaeon. Metope from Temple E at Selinus. Limestone covered with stucco, formerly painted; Artemis' flesh in marble, height 67³/₄″. c. 460 B.C. Museo Archeologico Nazionale, Palermo

Apollo. Head of a cult image. Marble, height 15¼". c. 470 B.C. From Cirò (Punta Alice). Museo Nazionale, Reggio di Calabria

The smooth planes of the head are all the more striking now that the original metal wig has been lost. This was part of an *acrolithic* (wood and marble) cult image. This eyes were inlaid in color.

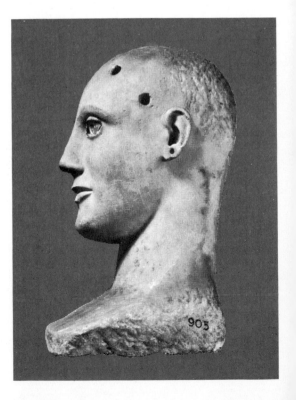

The impression conveyed by this head is badly falsified by the fact that it lacks the headdress which was originally of a different material—probably the goatskin characteristic of the goddess Juno Sospita (see page 123). The provenance of this head is not known, but it may originate from Lanuvium, the center where this goddess was chiefly worshiped.

Juno Sospita. Head of a cult image. Marble, eyes of chalcedony, eyelashes cut from bronze sheet, height 17⅝". c. 470 B.C. Vatican Museums, Rome

Heracles Seizing a Maiden. Back of a mirror. Bronze, diameter 7″. Beginning of fifth century B.C. British Museum, London

The inscriptions record the name of Heracles (Herecele) and of the maiden he is seizing (Mlacuch). The legend represented here seems to be a purely Etruscan one, and so has not been preserved in any written text. The flat relief approaches the finest Greek vase paintings in elegance; thus it may be presumed that the Etruscan artist was familiar with such compositions from the large number of imported Attic vases.

Athlete. Impression of intaglio on the base of a scarab. Carnelian, height ½″. Mid-fifth century B.C. Former State Museums, Berlin

This young man bending down to remove the dirt of the palaestra with his strigil bears the inscription TVTE, which probably equates him with the Greek hero Tydeus. His face is ringed by curly locks and his physique conforms fully to the Greek ideal. This scarab testifies to the high level of artistic achievement in Etruscan glyptic art.

This youth, whose head was part of a half life-size statue, exhibits a noble restraint that conforms to the ▶ early classical Greek ideal; but the delicate row of locks above his brow and the refined lingering, smile suggest an affinity with archaic art. The Etruscan artist was apparently unfamiliar with works from Magna Graecia; nevertheless the hair, held by a circlet at the nape of the neck, and the locks of hair on the brow accord with the Magna-Graecian fashion.

Head of a Youth. Bronze, height 36″.
c. 460 B.C. British Museum, London

Girl at a Chest. Clay, height 10¹/₄″. c. 460 B.C. From Locri. Museo Nazionale, Taranto

The large number of clay reliefs discovered at Locri are still markedly in the archaic tradition. Another characteristic feature is the predilection for detail, expressed here in the careful rendering of the chest; we can see depicted on it, as in a metope, the battle between Athena and Enceladus and a scene portraying satyrs and maenads.

The sepulcher chamber is decorated with scenes of feasting and gay dances, reflecting expectations of life in ▶ the Beyond. The bushes surrounding the revelers and dancers suggest a paradisiacal landscape. The old idea of a joyful afterlife has apparently not yet been abandoned, but in tomb paintings for post-archaic times it becomes ever rarer (see pages 140, 142, 167).

Banqueting Scene. Wall painting. c. 460 B.C. From the Tomba dei Leopardi ("Tomb of the Leopards"), Tarquinia. Museo Nazionale, Tarquinia

The high priest of Diana's sanctuary on Lake Nemi was invariably a fugitive who sought asylum there and defeated his predecessor in a duel. The representation in this relief is apparently related to the myth in which this custom originated. The Latin artist is still under the strong influence of late archaic Etruscan works, and has thus produced a highly individual variant of the Greek Ionic style. Surprising also is the marble (cf. page 54), which he is obviously inexperienced in working. Although the relief was discovered some two miles from the famous Diana sanctuary, it was probably erected there.

Cult legend from the sanctuary of Diana on Lake Nemi. Marble, 18⅞ x 30¼″. c. mid-fifth century B.C. From Aricia (Lake Nemi). Ny Carlsberg Glyptotek, Copenhagen

Birth of Aphrodite. Central part of the "Ludovisi Throne." Marble, 41 x 56¾". c. 460 B.C. From the Esquiline, Rome. Musco Nazionale Romano, Rome

The figure in the center and the two maidens supporting it as it emerges from the earth cannot be identified with certainty. But the representation clearly conveys the notion of death and rebirth to a new life probably originating in Pythagorean teaching. This was widely disseminated in Magna Graecia, the artist's homeland, but also found acceptance from an early date in Rome. This relief surmounted an altar whose voluted corners projected into spandrels left free for this purpose (see also pages 90f.).

A companion piece in Boston depicts a spirit making up its mind whether to enter the Elysian Fields with eternal youth or to return for another earthly existence with refreshed old age.

Female Flutist. Side panel of the "Ludovisi Throne." Marble, height 33¹/₈″. c. 460 B.C. From the Esquiline, Rome. Museo Nazionale Romano, Rome

The naked figure of the flutist is in stark contrast to the demurely clad bride on the opposite side of the monument. These two extremes probably indicate the two directions between which one could choose after rebirth, complementing the idea expressed in the image on the front (see page 89), just as the companion piece in Boston represents a youthful lyre player and an old woman. The side panels overlap the front and the rear of the altar.

Perseus and Medusa. From a tripod. Bronze, height 10⁷/₈″. c. 460 B.C. Museo Archeologico Nazionale, Florence

The eye is led in this plastic group, by way of a lion's claw and a broad ornamental band, down to the support. Perseus is staring straight ahead, and decapitating Medusa with a sickle, who sinks at his feet. On the pendant, which has survived, Peleus is wrestling with Thetis who is in the act of assuming animal form. The Etruscan artist here approaches the Greek style of the period very closely.

Amazon Torso. Clay with cream-colored slip and black and red color, height 8¹/₄″, width 14⁵/₈″. Beginning of fifth century B.C. From the Esquiline, Rome. Antiquarium Comunale, Rome

This Amazon, bleeding from a wound in the breast, is trying as she falls to shield herself from her enemy. This fragment formed part of a group which may have stood on the central *acroter* (pedestal on a pediment) in the decoration of a temple. Damophilus and Gorgasus are mentioned as Greek painters and clay sculptors active in Rome during the early fifth century; this torso, too, is the work of a Greek.

This she-wolf, symbolic of Rome, is looking around protectively as she suckles the twins Romulus and ▶ Remus (the figurines of these founders of the city were added at the end of the fifteenth century A.D.). The statue probably owes its existence to the national feeling aroused in the early days of the Republic after the expulsion of the Tarquins. The affinities with earlier Etruscan works (see page 62) are as unmistakable as the close stylistic links with the relief from Lake Nemi (see page 88). The slender, sinewy figure of the she-wolf, which as the animal sacred to Mars rescued his sons from destruction, is portrayed with an unusual flair for the essential quality of the animal.

She-wolf. Bronze, height 44⁷/₈", length 29¹/₂". Fifth century B.C. From Rome. Palazzo dei Conservatori, Rome

Horse's Head from a Dioscuri Group. Marble, height 22″, length of head 23¼″. c. 460 B.C. From the Forum Romanum, Rome. Antiquario Forense, Rome

The restrained modeling of this horse's head is also met with on Magna Graecian terra-cottas, and it is from this region that the artist originated. The group represents the two Dioscuri (Castor and Pollux, twin sons of Zeus) standing next to their horses, and was probably housed in the Temple of the Dioscuri (see page 202), next to which the fragments were discovered, and which was built as a token of gratitude for the assistance provided by the Dioscuri in the Battle of Lake Regillus (499 B.C.). The renewed supports under the belly of the horse show that this ancient work was piously maintained in a proper state of repair. It is assumed that the image was made in connection with the founding of the temple.

Apollo. Marble, height 60¹⁄₄″. c. 430 B.C. From the Temple of Apollo, Rome. Palazzo dei Conservatori, Rome

This Apollo, shooting an arrow from his bow, formed part of a group showing him and his sister Artemis killing the children of Niobe (see over). The figures probably stood upon a semicircular base, the gods in the center, the sons of Niobe on one side, and her daughters on the other. An artist from Tarentum made this group for the Temple of Apollo in Rome, pledged on the occasion of a plague and consecrated in 431 B.C.

Apollo and Diana, the avengers of their mother's violated honor, were regarded by the Romans as embodying the virtue of filial piety.

Niobid. Marble, height 58⅝″. c. 430 B.C. From the Esquiline, Rome. Museo Nazionale Romano, Rome

This daughter of Niobe, collapsing as she reaches for an arrow sticking in her back, probably stood on the right-hand end of the semicircular base (see page 95), in the center of which were the gods who were slaying them. Numerous small restorations show that this work was carefully looked after for a long time (see page 95). During the first century B.C. the group was, however, replaced at the temple with a newer one, and parts of the older one found their way into the possession of Roman collectors. Other Niobid statues from this group are to be found in Copenhagen and Berlin.

Head of a Young Man. Clay, height ▶ 6¼″. Mid-fifth century B.C. From Veii. Museo Nazionale di Villa Giulia, Rome

This head of a young man, in which the inspiration of Polycletus blends with Attic elegance, is nevertheless a characteristic work by an Etruscan artist, to whom we owe the sentimental, somewhat unclassical expression, reminiscent of Renaissance works, and the particular refinement of the head. There seems no longer to be any connection with earlier artistic traditions at Veii (see pages 62f.).

Young Man Praying. Bronze, height 7". c. 420 B.C. The Metropolitan Museum of Art, New York City

This statuette is clearly influenced by works of the Greek sculptor Polycletus. The motif in which one leg bears the weight while the other is given free play is employed with such assurance and so logically that one wonders whether this is not a Greek work. This statuette and similar works (see page 97 and opposite) are the products of Etruscan artists who wrestled intently with the innovations of post-archaic Greek art.

This terra-cotta statue, three-quarters life-size, shows that clay sculpture at Veii (see pages 62, 63) had broken with ancient tradition and was receptive to new impulses from Greece. The sculptures on the eastern pediment of the Temple of Zeus at Olympia were clearly taken as a model here.

Torso of a Young Man. Clay. Mid-fifth century B.C. From Veii. Museo Nazionale di Villa Giulia, Rome

Aeneas and Anchises. Clay, height 8¹/₈″. c. mid-fifth century B.C. From Veii. Museo Nazionale di Villa Giulia, Rome

The legend of the foundation of Rome begins with Aeneas' flight from Troy; the fact that he took his father Anchises with him was always regarded as symbolic of ancient Roman filial love. The discovery of two statuettes on this theme at Veii is surprising, especially from a period when Rome was entrenched before the gates of this mighty Etruscan city.

The style of this statuette differs from that of the torso of the young man (see page 99) by being very much more tradition-bound.

Hero. Clay, height 4³/4″. c. 460 B.C. Probably from Tarentum. Württembergisches Landesmuseum, Stuttgart

This bearded demigod wears a headband with a broad garland and a tall palmette. The head is a typical sample of Tarentine clay sculpture; it was produced from a mold, the details being added freehand.

Theseus Abandoning Ariadne. Clay with ▶
glaze paint. c. 430 B.C. From Gela. Museum of Fine Arts, Boston

Bearded Man. Clay, height 7³/₄″. Mid-fifth century B.C. Antikenmuseum, Collection Züst, Basel

The Etruscan artist has here transformed Magna-Graecian prototypes in an impressive way, giving the head a surprisingly profound expression. Like the melancholy manifest in the youth from Veii (see page 97), the resignation of this bearded man has no equivalent in Greek art; rather does it herald later Christian works.

This *stamnos* (wide-mouthed wine jar with horizontal handles at the shoulders) is an early sample of the ▶ painted vases, formerly imported from Greece, which were produced on a large scale in Lower Italy, probably under the stimulus of the foundation of the city of Thurii (443 B.C.). The composition of the picture and such details as Theseus' hair or the *hypnos* which makes Ariadne sleep more profoundly show that the painter has broken away from his Attic models. On the rear is depicted the dispatch of Bellerophon.

Reposing Couple. Vessel in the shape of a stag's head. Silver, height 7¹/₂″; traces of gilding. c. 430 B.C. From Tarentum. Museo Civico, Trieste

The neck of this drinking vessel is decorated with reliefs. The identification of the reposing couple (Boreas and Orithyia?) and of the man standing on the left (Erechtheus?) is uncertain; only Athena, to the right of the couple, is recognizable from her helmet and *aegis* (shield). The vessel is made from thick silver plate in repoussé work; the ears of the young fallow deer, the handle, and the rim have been soldered on.

From ancient Acragas, the Greek colony which Pindar praised as the most beautiful city of all, there have survived several temples arranged in a row upon a rocky terrace. Temple F, the so-called Temple of Concordia, is the best preserved of all Greek temples, except for the Theseum in Athens and the Temple of Hera at Paestum (see page 77). Together with the temple at Segesta (see overleaf), it is also the last Doric temple in Magna Graecia. After the defeat at the hands of the Carthaginians in 405 B.C. Acragas soon lost importance.

Temple F at Agrigento. Soft shell lime coated with stucco, 55′ 6″ x 129′ 4″. c. 425 B.C.

This temple, standing in remote hilly solitude, testifies to the prosperity enjoyed by the city of the Elymians during the fifth century B.C. on account of the Greek cities in its vicinity. The temple has no interior walls and also no plinths between those which now look like column bases; it remained unfinished because the affluence of the city suddenly died away toward the end of the century. This is why the columns have no flutings.

Temple at Segesta. Limestone, 75' 10" × 190' 4¹/₂". C. 420 B.C.

This head belonged to the statuette of a maiden, one-third life-size, the work of a Tarentine sculptor; as may be seen by comparing it with terra-cotta heads from Tarentum. The circumstances in which the statuette was discovered indicate with certainty that it did not find its way to Rome somewhat later as a piece of booty but was produced for a Roman as early as the fifth century B.C.

Head of a Maiden. Marble, height 3³/₄″. c. 450 B.C. From the Forum Romanum, Rome. Antiquario Forense, Rome

Goddess. Marble, height 32⅝″. c. 420 B.C. From Tarquinia. Former State Museums, Berlin

This goddess, fully draped, is shown pulling her mantle over the back of her head and raising it like a veil with her right hand while she supports herself upon a female idol executed in the ancient style. The style of this statuette is akin to that of Tarentine works, so that it may legitimately be considered as the product of a Greek artist working in Etruria. The following parts have been added since: the two hands and feet of the goddess; the face and left forearm of the idol; and most of the base.

Arethusa. Tetradrachm. Silver, diameter 1¹/₈″. After 413 B.C. Signed by Cimon. From Syracuse. Pennisi Collection

The head of Arethusa, the fountain nymph, appears in profile on other coins from Syracuse but only in this instance is she identified by an inscription. Cimon, whose signature is visible on the diadem, chose a three-quarter profile which allowed him to give the nymph a new expression, charming and animated. Together with Euainetus and Phrygillus, Cimon is among the greatest artists in the field of numismatic art which attained a particularly high standard in Sicily. The high degree of self-regard expressed in a coin of this kind seemed to be justified after the Athenians had been defeated off Syracuse. On the reverse of the coin, likewise signed by Cimon, is a quadriga with the horses galloping to the left.

FOURTH CENTURY B.C.

The century of civil war in Greece saw the Romans struggling in Italy with the Etruscans, Gauls, and Samnites, whom they overcame only after suffering bloody reverses. The old borders between Rome, Etruria, and Lower Italy gradually lost their divisive importance, and in the artistic field a self-sufficient world of Italic art arose. The imports into Etruria of Attic red-figure vases, still considerable during the fifth century, ceased as the need was met by domestic products and objects manufactured in Lower Italy. Artistic contacts between Magna Graecia and Etruria became fairly intensive, stimulating Etruscan artists to magnificent achievements. In Lower Italy the Hellenized native population came to the fore, causing a certain "barbarization" of art, a process which can be seen in Apulian, Campanian, and Lucanian vase painting. The Greek element in Lower Italy was strengthened by the activity of such Greek artists as Lysippus, who carved two well-known colossi, and by the foundation of the city of Thurii by the Athenians. But at the same time, other important cities fell into the hands of the Lucanians, Bruttians, Samnites, and Carthaginians, while dissensions raged among the Greeks themselves.

Political conditions in Greece and Italy led to the development of an Italic art which appears to be isolated from that of Greece and thrown back upon its own resources. In Rome, where in the civil strife the plebs improved its position, there prevailed an art blended of Etruscan and Greek elements

which corresponded to this state of compromise between social groups and to the beginnings of Roman hegemony over Italy.

This youthful head with a slight engraved beard continues the tradition of earlier Etruscan heads (see pages 97 f.). It gives an idea of the level of artistic achievement attained in Etruscan bronze statues; there was a large number of these, but later almost all of them were melted down. This head may well have belonged to a robed figure (see page 126).

Portrait Head. Bronze, height 9⁷/₈″. First half of fourth century B.C. From Lake Bolsena. British Museum, London

◀ *Medea's Revenge.* Apulian volute-crater. Clay with glaze paint and white and red color, height c. 15³/₄″. Fourth century B.C. From Canusium (Canosa). Staatliche Antikensammlung, Munich

Medea is shown slaying her children with the sword and Jason's wife with a poisoned garland; a chariot of snakes, driven by Oistros (fury), stands ready for her subsequent flight, which Jason, who appears from the right, cannot prevent. The center is occupied by the palace at Corinth in which the desperate King Creon holds up his daughter who is on the verge of collapse. The uppermost of the three registers is reserved for the gods. These magnificent large *craters* (mixing bowls) were designed for burials; the scenes represented on them bear witness to the great importance of the theater, especially at Tarentum.

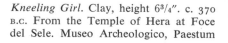

Kneeling Girl. Clay, height 6³/₄″. c. 370 B.C. From the Temple of Hera at Foce del Sele. Museo Archeologico, Paestum

This naked kneeling girl, spreading out her garment behind her with both hands, has not yet been satisfactorily explained despite the dove she is holding in her right hand and the two Eros-like figures upon her shoulder. It is perhaps too modern a notion to see in her a maiden commending herself to the protection of Hera before her marriage. However, the statuette is undoubtedly a votive offering.

One of the Dioscuri. Bronze, height including base 5⁵/₈″. Fourth century B.C. Museo Archeologico Nazionale, Florence ▶

This group, of a young man taming his horse, was probably one of a pair forming the ornament on a candelabrum. Thus we may identify the young man as either Castor or Pollux. He cannot be Alexander the Great with Bucephalus, since this work was produced before the Alexandrian age. It is one of the finest small Etruscan bronzes.

All four sides of this marble sarcophagus are covered with paintings which have been unusually well preserved. The exquisite workmanship and also the marble, which is unusual for Etruria, may indicate that the sarcophagus was by a Greek artist. But the *cist* (box) with engravings of the Argonauts (see page 116) also shows that scenes with a purely Greek effect could be produced outside the Greek lands. The inscription of the owner of the sarcophagus, Ramtha Huzcnai, is incised roughly into the paintings.

Amazon Battle. Scene on a sarcophagus. Painting upon marble, length of sarcophagus 76³/₈″. Fourth century B.C. From Tarquinia. Museo Archeologico Nazionale, Florence

Argonauts Among the Bebryces. Engraved cist. Bronze, height 20⁷/₈″, of frieze 8⁵/₈″. Fourth century B.C. Museo Nazionale di Villa Giulia, Rome

The inscription reads: NOVIOS PLAUTIOS MED ROMAI FECID DINDIA MACOLNIA FILEAI DEDIT ("Novius Plautius made [this cist] in Rome; Dindia Macolnia gave [it] to her daughter"). For the engraved frieze Novius Plautius no doubt used a Greek prototype which he altered negligibly. The Argonauts, in search of water, came into conflict with Amycus, the Bebrycian king, whom Polydeuces defeated in a pugilistic encounter. Besides the Argonauts, who can be identified all over the frieze—busy at the fountain, lying on the barque, or just watching—we can see a fleeing Nike, and Athena, and Boreas. This story is also represented on other monuments from Central Italy, but only in excerpts.

Maidens at Their Toilet. From an ▶ engraved cist. Bronze. Fourth century B.C. From Praeneste (Palestrina). Badisches Landesmuseum, Karlsruhe

This theme gives the artist an opportunity to represent clothed and unclothed maidens in a variety of postures. Without any regard for the pictorial scheme of the frieze, rings were affixed from which small chains were suspended (cf. page 17). These cists constitute a special group; they were found in Palestrina but may have originated in Roman workshops.

Nereid. Small altar. Clay, height 5⁷/₈″. Fourth century B.C. From the Forum Romanum, Rome. Antiquario Forense, Rome

This picture of a maiden seated upon a dolphin decorates, in the manner of a metope, the front of a small clay altar. The *arula* ("small altar") type is represented in Rome by numerous examples, most of which are closely linked to Apulian art.

Hunter and Maiden. Medallion on a bowl. Silver, diameter 6″. Fourth century B.C. From Barium (Bari). Museo Archeologico Provinciale, Bari

This representation was made under the influence of such famous works as the *Hermes* by Lysippus, but in its reticent mood it also reflects the impact of classical paintings. The figures may be of Meleager and Atalante, although there is no indication of the Calydonian boar hunt. The artist was concerned to represent not so much some legendary episode as a human encounter rich in meaning.

Silenus Grappling with a Serpent.
Bronze, height 17³/₈″. c. 350 B.C.
From Armentum. Staatliche An-
tikensammlung, Munich

This kneeling Silenus, striking with his sword a serpent clasped in his left hand, was formerly the support of a vessel. Similar supporting figures are depicted in Etruscan tomb paintings and were thus known in Etruria. The serpent was probably depicted coiled round the body of the vessel. The site where the statuette was found suggests that it was made in the border area between the Campanians and the Samnites. Silenus and other figures were later popular in Pompeii as supports for vessels and implements.

Athena and Enceladus. Ivory with traces of gilding, height of Athena 2⅝″. c. 350 B.C. From Paestum. Museo Archeologico, Paestum

The giant Enceladus is shown squatting upon an acanthus calyx, defending himself against Athena, who is lunging down at him with her lance; she herself stands upon a socle above a similar calyx. The irrational composition of this group suggests that the giant was placed directly beneath Athena in a column and that the latter crowned the shaft of it—interrupted by an acanthus calyx—even though her lance then pointed outward into space.

The playful element in this "acanthus column," the former function of which remains uncertain, also conforms to Etruscan taste. Several Etruscan candelabrum shafts show, for example, a man climbing up to reach safety from attack by a serpent.

Mars. Bronze, height 55⅞″. From Tuder (Todi). Vatican Museums, Rome

The inscription on one of the plates of the armor: AHAL TRUTITIS DUNUM DEDE ("Ahal Trutitis gave [it] as a gift"), indicates that this was a votive statue. It was discovered carefully embedded between four flagstones, i.e., it was buried deliberately. It had previously been in the open for a long time, as is shown by the trace of rust left by the iron spear upon the left thigh. This bronze statue, the only Etruscan one that is almost complete, thus owes its preservation to special circumstances. It remains uncertain whether it represents the god of war himself or a warrior. The helmet is missing.

Mercury. Clay with paint, height 4³/₄″. Fourth century B.C. From Falerii. Museo Nazionale di Villa Giulia, Rome

This small head was twisted sharply to the right in relation to the body. This fact, the upward gaze, and the very elaborate modeling of details, lend the small work a particular charm. The wings on the helmet have been broken off.

Juno Sospita. Head of a cult image. Marble, height 22″. Fourth century B.C. From Lanuvium. Lost

This head of the goddess, who wore a goatskin, may be the remains of an image for the new cult (see page 82) introduced by the Romans after conquering the town of Lanuvium (338 B.C.) when they made the Juno cult of Lanuvium into an official Roman one. Its large simple forms link it with the figure of Mars from Tuder (see opposite); the expression owes much to works by Leochares.

123

Chimaera. Part of a group. Bronze, height 31½″. Early fourth century B.C. From Arezzo. Museo Archeologico Nazionale, Florence

This wounded *chimaera* (she-monster, usually with a lion's head, goat's body, and serpent's tail), gazing upward, is only part of a group also including Bellerophon upon Pegasus; the form of the latter can be reconstructed from numerous Lower Italic vase paintings. The Etruscan inscription TINSCVIL on the right foreleg shows that the group was a votive offering. Since this chimaera was deliberately buried, together with other bronzes, it escaped destruction (see page 122), and today gives us an idea of the level reached by Etruscan art during the fourth century B.C. It was restored by Benvenuto Cellini in 1533 (the serpent's tail, one of the goat's horns, its beard, and the two legs on the animal's left side).

◄ *Female Head.* Clay, height 8⅞″. Fourth century B.C. From the garden at Santa Maria in Aracoeli, Rome. Palazzo dei Conservatori, Rome

This head bears a resemblance to a number of Etruscan votive heads, but differs from them in its unique hairstyle; the curls fall thickly upon the shoulder, while above the brow the hair is cut short. The shape of the face and the harsh expression also seem to suggest a peculiarly Roman element.

Portrait Statue. Clay, height 47¹/₄″. End of fourth century B.C. From Caere (Cerveteri). Vatican Museums, Rome

This Etruscan is wearing a toga which fits his body closely; standing in an erect posture, he manifests the self-confidence one associates with the Romans. This terra-cotta statue may to some extent compensate for the numerous bronze statues that have been lost (see page 122). The head was made from a mold of the original; it was then given finishing touches by hand to produce that essential resemblance to an individual person. The lower part of this statue is missing.

Lion. Stone. Fourth century B.C. From Val ▶ Vidone. Museo Archeologico Nazionale, Florence

This lion has just killed a ram and is looking around in triumph. It once stood upon the tomb of the Vevzna family. Along with the Arezzo chimaera (see page 125) and a large number of small bronzes, this lion, which surpasses all other works in monumental quality, shows the Etruscan artist's interest in the representation of animals.

Battle with Amazons. Detail from a sarcophagus. Stone. Fourth century B.C. From the Tomba delle Iscrizioni ("Tomb of the Inscriptions"), Vulci. Museo Nazionale di Villa Giulia, Rome

Between richly ornamented bands the battle between Heracles and the Amazons unfolds through a series of ▶ individual figures, pairs, and groups. Limestone reliefs of this kind were a speciality of Tarentum; they came from small sepulchral monuments.

◄ For this representation of a battle with the Amazons, which extends all around the sarcophagus, the artist uses ancient motifs from fifth-century Greek art. The same source probably inspired the curious terrain (or clouds?). On the right and left stand demons of death, and on the back of the sarcophagus a winged creature watches the bloody struggle across a similar undulating terrain.

Battle with Amazons. Frieze of a small sepulchral monument. Limestone, height 9⅞″. c. 350 B.C. From Tarentum. Museo Archeologico Nazionale, Taranto

Reposing Couple. From the lid of a sarcophagus. Marble, 84¹/₈ × 46¹/₂″. c. 350 B.C. From Vulci. Museum of Fine Arts, Boston

Scene at the Theater. Fragment of an Apulian calyx-crater. Clay with glaze paint and red and white color, height 8⅞″ (of entire vessel, formerly c. 19⅝″). c. 350 B.C. From Tarentum. Martin von Wagner Museum, Würzburg

Within lavish marble architecture, representing the scenery of a theater, are two figures opposite one another —probably Jason and Pelias. In the left wing of the palace, at a half-open door, a girl can be seen listening to the welcome given by the older man to the strange traveler. The absence of masks is striking. The passionate enthusiasm for the theater displayed by the people of Tarentum also finds expression in a number of other vase paintings (see page 148).

◄ Under a blanket which blossoms out like a calyx, as though the figures beneath were dancing, this couple embrace one another lovingly with the hope that the afterlife will be as blissful as the earthly one. Greek art was the means which enabled this master to represent the noble intimacy existing in a relationship between a man and a woman and at the same time to make it seem otherworldly. The body of the sarcophagus shows battle scenes involving Amazons, horsemen, and animals.

Head of Goddess. Marble, height 13³/₄". c. 340 B.C. From Tarentum. William Rockhill Nelson Art Gallery, Kansas City

This masterpiece by a Tarentine sculptor is in complete conformity with the ideal of Greek art of the time. In his delicate treatment of the marble, the artist has captured the essence of the female psyche, and reproduced the woman's gentle, wistful mood without detracting in any way from her majestic dignity.

Head of a Woman. Dark-brown clay, height 8⁷/₈″. End of fourth century B.C. From Caere (Cerveteri). Vatican Museums, Rome. Left: front view. Below: side view

The thick braids which cover the woman's head and frame her face, together with the refined severity of her expression, lend this portrait a character far superior to that of similar mass-produced votive heads. The head is modeled freehand from thick-walled clay, and may have served as a model for a bronze caster.

One of the Dioscuri. Bronze, height 17¾″. Toward the end of the fourth century B.C. Museo Nazionale, Naples

This young man, whose pointed hat suggests an identification as Castor or Pollux, has the slender proportions and flexibility of Lysippus' statues. One is reminded that at this very time Lysippus produced at Tarentum two colossi that are among his most famous works. This statuette is distinguished by its unusual size.

This oval container, in which toilet articles were found, is decorated in relief; between two palmette friezes there unfolds before us a lively Amazonomachy (Amazon battle). Since this was produced by stamping, the single scene is repeated three times. The handle is composed of a group of two persons mounted on swans; the legs have the shape of lions' claws.

Oval cist. Bronze, height 9¹/₂″. End of fourth century B.C. From Vulci. Vatican Museums, Rome

The acanthus scrolls sprouting at either side of an Eros in flight are adapted to the shape of the flask. The painter thus demonstrated his fine sense for the decorative effect of his gay motif.

This sarcophagus, imitating an altar in ▶ shape, is decorated at the corners of the lid with volutes growing out of acanthus bracts as well as with a monumental frieze of metopes and triglyphs below a row of dentils. The inscription, which replaces an earlier shorter one, refers to the consul of 298 B.C. and is a eulogy in early Latin Saturnian verse upon the official career and deeds of this Scipio.

Sarcophagus of L. Cornelius Scipio Barbatus. Grayish-green volcanic tufa with white and black veins, 55⁷/₈ × 109". Beginning of third century B.C. From Scipio's tomb on the Via Appia, Rome. Vatican Museums, Rome

THIRD CENTURY B.C.

According to Livy, Rome would have been able to repel an attack upon Italy by Alexander the Great, so strong had her position become as mistress of the peninsula. It was further enhanced by the final defeat of the Gauls, the victory over the Carthaginians, and the success against Pyrrhus who had sought to carve out an empire for himself in Italy. Rome was therefore a power to be reckoned with in the politics of the ancient world.

Her position as a cultural center owed much to the poets who came to reside there, such as Livius Andronicus from Tarentum, Naevius from Campania, Ennius from Apulia, Plautus from Sarsina in Umbria, and Caecilius from Celtic Milan. Pictorial art in Italy was, too, wholly under the sway of the Romans, who began to strike coins and have their triumphs recorded in paintings.

The convulsions unleashed by Alexander the Great in the Greek world of the East were not without effect upon Italy. Emulation of Alexander went beyond the fashion of shaving one's beard. Art was reinvigorated by Greek influences. The broadening of men's intellectual horizons, which Alexander brought about, also drew Italy and Greece into closer contact, and thus Rome, too, after a period of isolation, intensified her relations with Greece. In 292 B.C., Q. Ogulnius brought the statue of Asclepius from Epidaurus to Rome and provided the god with a new home on the island in the Tiber. But the Romans' increased self-confidence led

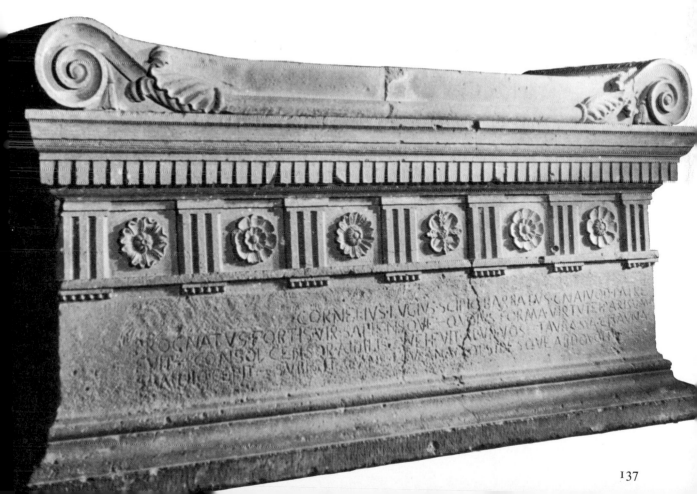

them to reflect upon their own past: in 296 B.C., the same Q. Ogulnius, with his brother Gnaeus, erected a statue of the Roman she-wolf, and Roman coins also feature Lupa with Romulus and Remus.

In Etruria the loss of political independence was followed by an astonishing economic upsurge which also brought about a burst of artistic activity. In Magna Graecia, on the other hand, political decline went hand in hand with artistic desolation in the Greek cities.

When the Romans toward the end of the century were suddenly made aware of the beauty and cultural worth of Greek art through the booty brought from Syracuse, a trend which had long been of increasing importance reached its climax. The "barbarization" of the Greeks was thus offset by the hellenization of the Italic peoples—a development of far-reaching historical significance.

This hand-modeled head, with its disheveled hair and sober expression, expresses the new ideal that came to the fore with Alexander the Great. The turn of the head and the mimicry of the face reproduce the qualities of the model in a virtuoso fashion. The statue to which this head belonged must have been full of life.

Head of a Young Man. Clay, height 9½″. Third century B.C. From Caere (Cerveteri). Vatican Museums, Rome

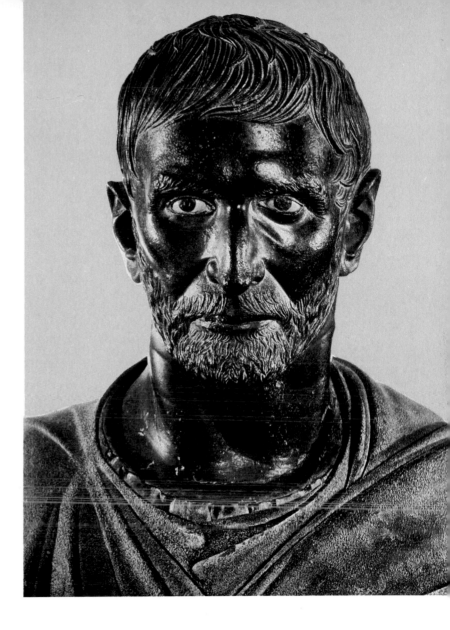

Portrait of a Roman. Bronze with white and brownish-red inlays in the eyes, height 12⅝". Beginning of third century B.C. From Rome. Palazzo dei Conservatori, Rome

The old identification of this portrait as one of Brutus is untenable: it seems rather to embody all the Roman virtues. A probable model would have been M. Curius Dentatus, who as consul in 290 B.C. was victorious over the Samnites; but the much-admired head, which by some lucky chance escaped destruction, far more likely portrays some unknown Roman of the time.

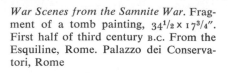

War Scenes from the Samnite War. Fragment of a tomb painting, 34¹/₂ × 17³/₄". First half of third century B.C. From the Esquiline, Rome. Palazzo dei Conservatori, Rome

In three registers, divided only by a fine line, are represented the surrender of a city, the negotiations between the two commanders, and a battle. M. Fannius, dressed in non-Roman style with a splendid helmet, appears twice; the Roman, Q. Fabius, wears the toga. The two men may not necessarily be historical personalities, but the latter may be Q. Fabius Maximus Rullianus (dictator in 315 B.C.).

This bust represents a woman who has none of the lightness found in earlier portraits of a similar kind (see page 133); she looks almost Roman. The hair is combed close to the head and held together by a knot at the nape of the neck; only over the brow is it brushed upward slightly. The delicate lion's-head earrings accentuate the austerity of this dutiful woman, portrayed here with marked sympathetic insight. One shoulder of the bust is missing.

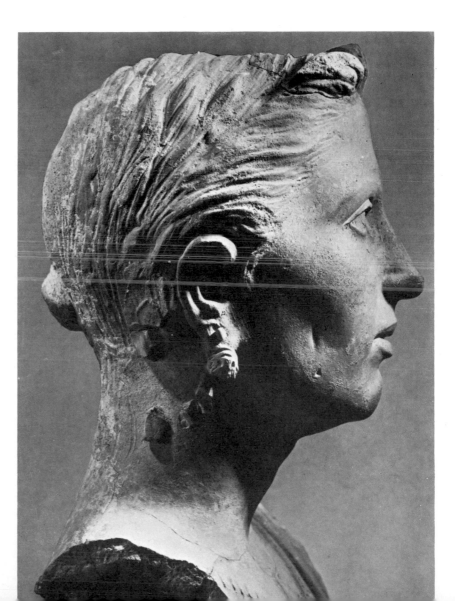

Portrait of an Elderly Woman. Clay, height 13³/₄″. Third century B.C. From Caere (Cerveteri). Vatican Museums, Rome

Among the groups of duelers and the like two are of special interest: in one Macstrna is shown freeing Caile Vipinas; in the other Marce Camitlnas is slaying Cneve Tarchunies Rumach. The latter is to be understood as the Roman king Tarquinius, who was apparently killed when freeing some captives. The Macstrna who liberates Caelius Vibenna is known to us under a different name as the Roman king, Servius Tullius. Inside the tomb this frieze was a companion piece to a representation of the sacrifice of Trojan prisoners at the tomb of Patroclus (see page 146).

Battle Scenes from the Roman Imperial Period. Wall painting. Height 65³/₈". Beginning of third century B.C. From the Tomba François ("François Tomb"), Vulci. Villa Torlonia, Rome

Woman's Head. c. 300 B.C. From the Tomba dell'Orco ("Tomb of Hades"), Tarquinia

This impressive portrait of a woman is from a banqueting scene which shows Arnth Velcha beside his wife, whose name, Velia, is added. The painter has represented the "classical" and yet typically Etruscan profile very effectively in a light color against a dark background; this ends arbitrarily, as it seems, in a wavy line, and the woman's brown hair is set off to advantage against a lighter ground.

Within a lavishly decorated frame this elephant is striding by followed by a young one. From the battlements ▶
of the turret on its back soldiers can be seen hurling down lances; on the animal's neck sits its driver with his
characteristic goad. The elephants introduced into Italy for military purposes by Pyrrhus greatly stirred the
imagination of Italic artists. The native artist used for this unique painting a technique commonly employed
in Lower Italy (see page 148).

Elephant. Figured vessel. Clay, height 13³/₄″. Third century B.C. From
Pompeii. Museo Nazionale, Naples

This animal, whose use in warfare is
clear from the turret on its back, has
a Negro driver feeding his charge at
the same time. The statuette is open
at the top and was probably used as
a vessel.

War Elephant and Calf. Polychrome plate. Clay with glaze paint and lavish use of red and white color, height 2¹/₄″, diameter 11⁵/₈″. First half of third century B.C. From the Necropoli delle Macchia, Leprignano (Capena). Museo Nazionale di Villa Giulia, Rome

◄ *Patroclus' Shade.* From a wall painting in the Tomba François ("François Tomb"), Vulci. Early third century B.C. Villa Torlonia, Rome

Patroclus' shade (Hinthial Patrucles) is shown watching Trojan prisoners being sacrificed at his tomb (see page 142). His bowed head, framed by almost purple locks, reflects grace as well as sorrow.

Head of a Young Man. Clay. Early third century B.C. From the Esquiline, Rome. Ashmolean Museum, Oxford

This head of a young man with short locks was probably part of a seated figure; he is shown leaning his head upon his left hand, his sublime gaze directed upward. This mood, evidently related to the meaning of the work (not known), connects it with Greek and late classical art.

On the front of this calyx-crater an actor, playing the part of a slave and holding a small table in his hands, is running toward banqueting guests (not represented). He is wearing the typical mask and thick jerkin associated with the *phlyax* farce. On the other side the only ornamentation is an ivy scroll.

Apulian crater. Clay with glaze paint and white and red color, height 11¹/₈″. Third century B.C. From Fasano (Egnatia). British Museum, London

Youth in a Cloak. Clay, height 71⅝". Third century B.C. From Pignataro, Campania. Ny Carlsberg Glyptotek, Copenhagen

Many life-size terra-cotta statues have been discovered in Campanian sanctuaries. Their motifs, taken from fourth-century Greek art, show a fairly marked tendency toward the primitive. This statue of a youth, now in Copenhagen, is one of those that typify the best of this tradition.

Head of a Youth. Clay, height 9½". Early third century B.C. From Antemnae, Rome.
Museo Nazionale di Villa Giulia, Rome

This head, modeled in a lively manner, comes from the immediate vicinity of Rome (Antemnae lost its independence at an early date). It proves that the art of clay sculpture, known from Falerii (see page 159), was not restricted to that site. The head is badly damaged. Small fragments of a similar kind have also been found on the Palatine Hill.

Head of a Priest (?). Bronze, height 8¹/₄″. Third century B.C. From the environs of Rome. British Museum, London

The close-fitting cap, evidently worked in leather and fastened beneath the chin by a strap, leaving the ears uncovered, suggests that this young man might be a *flamen* (Roman priest), although the characteristic feature of such sacerdotal caps, an upright pointed tag (see page 205), is missing here. It therefore may be an athlete's cap or the lining for a helmet. The head, cast independently, was attached to a statue; the eyes were indicated by colored inlays.

Rape of Persephone. Relief-style limestone group, height 15³/₈″.
Third century B.C. From Tarentum. Museo Nazionale, Taranto

Hades, carrying Persephone upon his shoulder, is shown moving away sharply to the left, while a horrified
playmate flees in the opposite direction. Two girls on the left and others on the right pick up the movement,
so increasing the impression of confusion and fear. These figures are worked in the round and stood against
the background of a pediment. The feet and the base are missing.

These surviving fragments of painting from a sepulchral chamber are noteworthy for their elongated figures shown in violent movement. The painter laid more stress upon graphic narrative effect than upon detailed working of his figures, sketched out in a rough fashion.

Battle Scenes. Fragment of a wall painting. 30¹/₄ × 49¹/₄″. Third century B.C. From the Esquiline, Rome. Palazzo dei Conservatori, Rome

This battle with Amazons, in which the groups of figures are widely spaced, decorates the body of a chestlike sarcophagus; on the lid, the semirecumbent figure of Velthur is represented. Several third-century Etruscan sarcophagi feature such "classical" battle scenes as well as scenes drawn from Etruscan life or associated with the voyage to the Beyond.

Battle with Amazons. From the sarcophagus of Velthur Partunus. Limestone with traces of paint. Third century B.C. From Tarquinia. Museo Nazionale, Tarquinia

Girl Running. Metope. Limestone, height 28″. Third century B.C. "Italic Temple," Paestum

These metopes, which are generally thought to have belonged to a building of the first century B.C., probably stem from a temple, the *Capitolium* of the Roman colony Paestum (from 273 B.C.) which cuts into a theater-like structure *(Comitium)*. The style in which they are executed points, however, to an earlier date. It is, moreover, improbable that this impressive public building should only have been built two hundred years later.

These statuettes of Gauls remind us of the threat posed to Italy by these invaders from the north who conquered Rome (387 B.C.) and traversed the peninsula until they were finally defeated near Clastidium (222 B.C.). They also suffered a defeat at Telamon in 225 B.C.

Defeated Gaul. Bronze, height 4³/₄″. Third century B.C. From Telamon. Museo Archeologico Nazionale, Florence

Defeated Gaul. Bronze, height 5³/₈″. Third century B.C. From Rome. Former State Museums, Berlin

Orpheus Surrounded by the Animals.
Peperino, height 35³/₈″. Third century
B.C. From the vicinity of the Porta
Tiburtina, Rome. Palazzo dei Conser-
vatori, Rome

This sculpture, probably from a
tomb, represents Orpheus, singing with lyre accompaniment,
surrounded by animals enchanted
by his music. One can identify a
little owl, a lion, a panther, and a
hare. The choice of theme is
probably linked with the Orphic
mysteries. Orpheus' absorption in
his singing is rendered very com-
pellingly and his youthful, care-
free attitude brings out the intimacy of the scene.

Head of a Maenad. Tufa, height 11⅝″. Third century B.C. Vatican Museums, Rome

This head blends classical Greek form with Etruscan sentiment and delight in worldly beauty. The *maenad* (frenzied female participant in the Dionysian rites), ecstatically gazing upward in search of the god Dionysus, is wearing a garland of ivy and earrings each consisting of a round disk with a pyramid-shaped pendant.

This head with its classical reserve exemplifies a more conservative trend than the Apollo and the other heads on the same pediment. The right side has been sketchily treated, suggesting that the head was originally turned toward the right.

Female Head. Clay with brown paint, height 7⁷/₈″. Early third century B.C. From Falerii (Città Castellana). Museo Nazionale di Villa Giulia, Rome

Appliqué reliefs. Gilded clay, height 3¹⁄₈″. Early third century B.C. From Tarentum. Museo Nazionale, Taranto

These gilded clay reliefs, with the background cut away, were used to decorate wooden sarcophagi. They represent men reposing or making music, *Erotes* (cupids), and satyrs, as well as men in combat and legendary beasts. They are closely akin to the Tarentine limestone reliefs (see page 152).

The peculiar shape of this vessel, the stopped-out ornament, and the bluish color of the glaze paint identify ▶ this *cantharus* (deep, stemmed cup with loop-shaped handles continuing the curve of the bottom of the body upward) as an Etruscan work; the nearest parallels to the style of applied relief decoration are in Lower Italic art. The applied molded reliefs show Nereids riding across the sea upon sea horses and carrying weapons of Achilles, Heracles, a female dancer, and two reclining youths. The artist was obviously more concerned to produce a spectacular and gay effect than to convey a sharply focused scene.

Cantharus with applied relief decoration. Clay with glaze paint, white color, and applied clay reliefs (painted in blue and red and partly gilded), height 9¼″. Early third century B.C. Former State Museums, Berlin

Here, as on tombs (see below and page 237) and Etruscan cinerary urns, for example, the motif of the Nereid ▶
riding across the sea symbolizes a cheerful existence beyond human misery. It is significant that this theme
not only serves to point to the life after death, but also decorates everyday utensils such as the shell-shaped
pyxis from which this relief comes (see also page 161).

Triton and Nereids. Marble, height 32⅝″. Second half of third century B.C. From Rome. Staatliche Antikensammlung,
Munich

These Nereids are taking part with others in the wedding procession of Poseidon and Amphitrite. This scene
appears on three sides of the work, the fourth (in the Louvre, Paris) depicting a Roman theme (Suovetauri-
lian sacrifice). These reliefs probably originate from the tomb of a man who had a decisive share in winning
Rome's maritime supremacy, symbolized by the wedding of the sea-gods. One is reminded in the first place
of C. Lutatius Catulus and his victory in 241 B.C.; the "Sepulchrum Lutatiorum" was situated on the right
bank of the Tiber.

Nereid Riding a Sea Dragon. Lid of a pyxis. Silver, partly gilded, a red stone for the dragon's eye, diameter 4″. Third century B.C. From Canusium (Canosa). Museo Nazionale, Taranto

Head of a Young Man. Clay, height 11 3/4". Third century B.C. Danish National Museum, Copenhagen ▶

As is usually the case with Etruscan votive portraiture, this head is produced from a mold. It is distinguished by the emotionally expressive turn of the head and the abundant locks. In this mass-produced portrait, of which several copies are known, the ideal of Scopas lives on.

This demon in the guise of a swan is probably a wind-god, possibly Zephyrus; the traveler whom he refreshes with a cool drink from his jug may be Jason and the ram skin on his back the "Golden Fleece." This group is unmatched in the daring of its composition, which we again encounter in Tarentine terra-cottas, as well as in its compact movement and exquisite execution. It is not surprising that Etruscan bronze statuettes were already held in particularly high esteem by Roman art collectors. The shaft under the traveler's arm is missing; the base is ancient but not original.

Bird-Demon Refreshing a Traveler. Bronze, height 15". Third century B.C. Museo Archeologico Nazionale, Florence

Three men in strange clothing are holding a pig and beating it with sticks; behind them is an image of Mars. ▶
This is probably a military agreement being ratified by a ritual act. The god was to smite the defaulter in the
same way as "I strike this pig today"—so ran the oath (Livy, I, 23–25). Similar sacrifices of pigs are depicted
upon third-century Roman coins and gems.

This ram, which with a companion piece adorned a gate in the fortress of Syracuse during the Middle Ages,
was much admired by Goethe. He saw both of them in Palermo and called them "mighty figures from mythol-
ogy, worthy of bearing Phrixus and Helle. " The original significance of this pair of rams is unknown, as is the
purpose which they formerly served. One of them was destroyed by a cannonball during the revolution of
1848. On this one the tail, left ear, and part of the left hind leg have been restored.

Ram. Bronze, 30¹/₄ × 53¹/₈″. Third century B.C. From Syracuse. Museo Archeologico Nazionale, Palermo

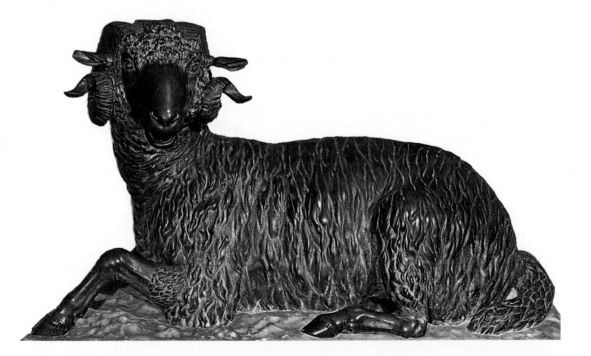

Cult Act. Mosaic copy, made in Imperial times, of a third-century B.C. original painting. 35³/₈ × 35³/₈″. Museo Borghese, Rome

The arch is flanked by pilasters. Above is a loggia, with latticework and figures looking out: Tinia (Jupiter) in the center, Castor and Pollux to the left and right, and at either end a horse. In each of the spandrels there was a head, but only one of these has survived. Similar decorations are also found on Etruscan cinerary urns.

Etruscan town gate (Porta Marzia) in Perugia. Early second century B.C. Built into the sixteenth-century fortifications by Antonio da Sangallo

SECOND CENTURY B.C.

The first half of this century, the age of Q. Flamininus, the Scipios, and Aemilius Paulus, is dominated by the conflicts between Rome and the Greek princes. The well-tried alliance with Pergamon had as a consequence the strong influence which the art of Pergamon exerted upon that of Rome. The vast quantities of examples of Greek art which found their way to Rome as booty, especially those which figured in L. Scipio's triumphal procession after his victory over Antiochus, made it so familiar in Rome that toward the middle of the century the city became the focal point for Greek artists.

During Alexander's reign Greek art had to adapt itself to the taste of the Macedonians, and, under his successors, to oriental requirements. It was entirely in the service of the princes, and it was only a logical consequence of the complete shift in the balance of power in Rome's favor that the artists of the time, along with the streams of plunder, turned toward Rome. From there artistic influences spread outward to Etruria and Lower Italy. In Etruria the influence of Pergamon was especially noticeable, since its baroque forms were highly suited to the Etruscan love of fine curved lines and ebullient presentation. Classical models, on the other hand, were adopted only with reluctance, since classicist tendencies had always been alien to the Etruscans; if they occurred at all, then it was probably only from a desire to imitate Rome's example. In parts of Lower Italy the artistic influences radiating from Rome fell upon more fertile ground, as for example, to a certain extent in Pompeii, where the Samnites kept Greek traditions alive. The painting of the *Battle of Alexander the Great,* which was presumably exhibited in Rome at this time, exerted much less influence upon Etruscan art than it did upon that of Lower Italy, to which we are indebted for the mosaic copy from Pompeii.

After the Roman Empire had been firmly established with the subjugation of Spain, Carthage, Greece, and Asia Minor, and the entire artistic heritage of Greece had come to be concentrated in Rome, "modern" (post-Alexandrian) art was probably of greater importance than ancient "classical" art. Last but not least, the "Attalid heritage" (133 B.C.) was to force the baroque trend once again to the fore.

The serpent-footed giant is painted on two sides of the center pillar supporting the ceiling of the tomb, and seems to be bearing its weight. The theme and some details of this painting bring to mind the huge altar frieze at Pergamon.

Winged Giant. On the center pillar of the Tomba del Tifone ("Tomb of Typhon"), Tarquinia. Second century B.C.

This naked goddess, standing beside a tree upon which she has suspended her robe, is drying her hair after a bath. The style corresponds to that of the pediment from Città Alba (see opposite).

Venus. From an antefix. Clay with traces of red, white, and blue paint, height 15³/₄″. From the Forum Romanum, Rome. Antiquario Forense, Rome

Ariadne and the Thiasus of Dionysus. From a pediment. Clay, height 37″. From Cività Alba. Museo Civico, Bologna

Satyrs (gods of the woods) and *maenads* have found Ariadne asleep and are drawing their master Dionysus' attention to her. The striking combination of figures in the round against a background, as well as the violent movements, recall third-century Tarentine reliefs (see page 152). The composition is characteristic of Etruscan pediments, in which the tricky problem of filling a steep triangle with terra-cotta figures was solved in a masterly way, which was probably also carried over into pediments of Imperial times (see page 227).

Eagle with Palm of Victory and Wreath. Sardonyx with one white and one brown layer, diameter 8⁵/₈″. Shortly after 190 B.C. Kunsthistorisches Museum, Vienna

Shield with the Helmeted Head of a Goddess. From a victory monument with relief decoration. Bluish gray, very fine limestone, diameter 20¹/₂″. Early second century B.C. From the slope of the Capitol Hill, Rome. Palazzo dei Conservatori, Rome

The attractive precision of the ornamentation and the sober rendering of the weapons blend the Roman sense of reality with the art of Pergamon known from the friezes of weapons there. It is not possible to identify exactly the victory commemorated by this monument, on which other weapons appear, some of them (armor, greaves) pointing to Heracles and others (shield) to the Dioscuri. It may be identical with that erected by Scipio before his departure for Asia (190 B.C.), possibly to mark his victory at Zama in 202 B.C.

◄ Within an egg-and-dart border (and in a sixteenth-century setting), Zeus' eagle fits harmoniously within the round shape of the stone. This precious cameo, whose unique style suggests that it is from Pergamon, probably found its way to Rome as a gift from Eumenes II to Publius Scipio Africanus Maior as a token of gratitude after the Battle of Magnesia near Mount Sipylus (190 B.C.). The symbolic rendering of victory, which avoids any personal glorification of the victor, is in accordance with Roman ideas.

Medusa. Bronze, height 6¹/₄″. Second century B.C. From the Palazzolo Acreide (Acrae). Museo Nazionale, Syracuse

The Medusa who once was turned to stone has here become a sentimental female being, engrossed in her thoughts as if dreaming. She wears a scaly breastplate.

Head with Phrygian Cap. Clay, traces of red on the cap, height 5″. Vatican Museums, Rome

Several figures were probably combined in a high relief (see page 171); the Phrygian cap may identify this young man as Paris. Other heads have been preserved, among them that of an old woman, possibly Hecuba. The style suggests the influence of the art of Pergamon, as manifest in the great altar frieze.

175

Head of a Goddess from a cult image.
Marble, height 59″. Second century B.C.
From the temples in Largo Argentina.
Palazzo dei Conservatori, Rome

From the turn of the head and the arm, the two pieces that have been preserved, it may be concluded that this cult statue depicted a goddess in movement. The draped parts of her body were probably of wood, since no remains of them have survived. Her identity is unknown.

This bronze head, which with its long hair and "necklets of Venus" at the throat looks so feminine, probably represents Apollo and was part of a statue, the theme of which was similar to the *Apollo Belvedere;* the latter's divinity has here yielded to a somewhat theatrical pose.

Head of Apollo. Bronze, height 19⅝". Second century B.C. From the sea near Salerno. Museo Provinciale, Salerno

This moving representation of an elderly couple is a masterpiece of late Etruscan clay sculpture. The sober expression of the man and the woman's drawn face are far removed from the air of happiness that once prevailed (see page 56). A coiffure similar to the woman's was worn later by Livia, Augustus' consort.

Reposing Couple. Group on the lid of a cinerary urn. Clay, $16^{1}/_{8} \times 28''$. Second century B.C. From Volterra. Museo Guarnacci, Volterra

Reposing Couple. Figure on capital of pilaster. Tufa, 19 × 30³/₈″. Second century B.C. From the Casa dei Capitelli Figurati ("House of Figured Capitals"), Pompeii. Antiquarium, Pompeii

The entrances to the early Samnite houses at Pompeii, which have a noble simplicity, are frequently decorated with figured capitals above the pilasters either side. The combination of human busts and heads with capitals is also frequently encountered in Etruria and at Tarentum. Here we have another example of the ancients' readiness to employ the human figure ornamentally (see pages 60, 121).

Procession. Detail from paintings in the Tomba del Tifone ("Tomb of Typhon"), Tarquinia. Second century B.C.

This procession of men striding down toward Hades in an unconstrained manner, though closely grouped together, led by demons of death, is unfortunately in a poor condition. It invites comparison with the *Ara Pacis* (see page 190), the processional frieze of which apparently continues an ancient Italic tradition.

FIRST CENTURY B.C.

The end of the second century was overshadowed by the revolt of the Gracchi and by the Cimbric and Teutonic invasions. Even after this there was no peace: the Social War and the civil strife between Marius and Sulla, Pompey and Caesar, the wars against Mithridates, the suppression of the slaves and pirates, and finally the struggles that followed Caesar's assassination—all of these events shook Rome; nevertheless the city continued to be adorned with splendid marble temples, theaters, squares, and statues. Moreover, the classicist trend in art seems to have gained ground, all the more so since the collection of precious works and the appearance of writings on the theory of art demonstrate the growth of the Romans' interest in the art of the remoter past. In Pompeii, alongside the final paintings of the late Greek period, there are, significantly, copies based upon classical models—and this probably even before Pompeii had become a Roman military colony (80 B.C.). In 88 B.C. all Italic peoples received Roman citizenship, including the Etruscans whose art lost all significance. Plutarch states that a plaintive trumpeting announced the end of the Etruscan era (*Sulla*, 7). Roman citizenship was also conferred upon Pasiteles, the Greek artist from Lower Italy who exerted a decisive influence on the art of his day; his gold and ivory Jupiter in the Temple of Metellus was famous. Arcesilaus worked for Caesar and Lucullus as well as for the collectors Asinius Pollio and Varro. Apollonius produced the gold and ivory cult image for the reconstructed Temple of Jupiter on the Capitol Hill after this had burned down; and two artists from Tralles, Apollonius and Tauriscus, created the marble group of statuary, in Asinius Pollio's collection, representing Zethus, Amphion, Dirce, and the Bull. Such information, as well as the mere mention of the golden statues on the Capitol showing Sulla's capture of Jugurtha, and his signet ring with the same scene, or the paintings done for the theater and for triumphs—all this conveys a far better impression of Roman art during the late Republic than most of the surviving monuments, such as the numerous busts on grave stelae with their rather primitive and misleading workmanship.

Boxer. Bronze, height 50³/₈″. First century B.C. From the Via Nazionale, Rome. Museo Nazionale Romano, Rome

This boxer, exhausted by the fight, is taking a rest. Although beaten, he looks defiantly over his shoulder. This figure may represent a mythical pugilist, such as Amycus (see page 116), who was worsted by Polydeuces.

The blocklike compactness of the composition is effectively broken by the sharp turn of the head. The marks of blows on the face of this professional pugilist and his heavy *cestus* ("boxing gloves") indicate the harshness of his sport.

In accordance with Greek custom, mosaic floors were used to embellish dwellings, and their walls were covered with painted stucco to imitate a facing of precious stones. The picture of the tiger, on whose back sits a small winged Dionysus, is surrounded by a garland of masks and a wavy band. During this period there was a fashion for easily comprehensible allegory and it was permitted to show the god Dionysus as a child with the wings of Eros.

Architectural composition. Height 96¹/₈″. c. 50 B.C. From the bedchamber in the villa at Boscoreale. The Metropolitan Museum of Art, New York City ▶

Dionysus Riding the Tiger. Mosaic, 33¹/₂ × 33¹/₂″. Early first century B.C. From the Casa del Fauno ("House of the Faun"), Pompeii. Museo Nazionale, Naples

This fanciful representation of houses towering one above the other with their balconies, stairways, small temples, and colonnades, hardly corresponds to reality, even in a capital city like Rome, the many-storied apartment blocks of which were notorious. This must rather be a stage set, as is indicated by the comic mask on the upper border. In 99 B.C. birds are said to have tried to perch upon stage scenery with similar illusionistic painting in Rome.

Sacrificial Scene. c. 60 B.C. Villa dei Misteri ("Villa of the Mysteries"), Pompeii

A hall in this villa, situated outside the walls of Pompeii, is painted with a frieze of twenty-nine life-size figures showing preparations for a wedding and scenes from the Mysteries; these are combined in a strange way with realistic scenes depicting groups of nature spirits as well as Dionysus and Ariadne. Thus the figure of the ancient Silenus is to be found standing next to the sacrificial scene in which the priestess sits with her back to the viewer. Probably only initiates understood completely the meaning of the frieze, the original creation of an important artist and an integral part of the room it served to decorate.

The decoration of the Casa dei Grifi belongs to the earliest fashion, also known from Pompeii, whereby light stucco relief and appropriate painting were used to make the walls look as though they were covered with expensive stone. A surprising feature here is the heraldic griffin in the lunette, set off against the background in stucco in low relief.

Wall decoration. Early first century B.C. From the Casa dei Grifi ("House of the Griffins"), on the Palatine Hill, Rome

Small sepulchral temple. Limestone, height 26′ 6″. First century B.C. (?). Agrigentum, to the south of the temple terrace

This small temple, with Ionic columns at the corners and a Doric frieze, stands upon a cubic base. The false doors between the columns were already a favorite motif in archaic Etruscan tomb paintings, and also in the wall decoration of houses in that period (see page 183). As a hero, the deceased resides high above mortal visitors. The dating of the tomb, which was probably crowned by a stepped pyramid, is most uncertain; it may originate from the third or second century B.C.

This statue, signed by Agasias, the son of Dositheus from Ephesus, takes a prototype from the Alexandrian ▶ era and turns it into an ideal heroic image. The young man is fighting a mounted opponent, not depicted here, and straining every muscle in a ferocious lunge. The person who commissioned the work was probably a Roman who may have put it straight into his collection.

Heroic Warrior. Marble, height 61″. Early first century B.C. Formerly in the Borghese Collection, Rome. The Louvre, Paris

The *Odyssey* landscapes. Height 54³/₄″. First century B.C., probably based upon an earlier prototype. From the Esquiline, Rome. Vatican Library, Rome:

The *Odyssey* landscapes—a sequence of individual pictures between pillars dividing up a wall—devote more space than is usual to bays, rocks, vegetation, and sky. Late Greek epic poetry, in contrast to Homer, contained detailed descriptions of the landscapes in which the heroes' adventures took place. The figures featured in the *Odyssey* and the numerous personifications of places have had their names added in Greek.

Three Companions of Odysseus Encountering the Daughter of Antiphatis, King of the Laestrygones (Odyssey, X, 100 ff.)

The Laestrygones Attacking Odysseus' Ships (Odyssey, X, 119 ff.)

THE AGE OF AUGUSTUS (27 B.C.–A.D. 14)

The art of the Augustan age was definitive for the whole of the Imperial period. Through a genuine synthesis of the restrained art of Greece with the older Italic art—including that of Magna Graecia—there arose a new art which fitted the Roman ideal as Augustus understood it. The oft cited verses of Virgil show that in artistic matters, however, the Romans left the dominant role to the Greeks. Insofar as baroque exuberance and rococo decadence were not wholly excluded, art was held within a framework of strict conventions, and it was through the interplay between its inner dynamism and these narrow external limits that artists often evolved a marked virtuosity.

The incorporation of Egypt into the Roman Empire (30 B.C.) provided new stimuli—Egyptianizing elements which made themselves felt especially in mural decoration, though the flourishing art of cutting cameos in stone was also undoubtedly linked with this political development.

Pictorial art and poetry cross-fertilized each other too. Much of the verse of Virgil, Horace, or Ovid finds some counterpart under the forms of painting, sculpture, or reliefs. But behind all these expressions of art, one can discern the guiding spirit of Augustus, whose own personality stamped the age. Augustan art is distinguished for the utmost subtlety and delicacy of execution, for restraint in medium, form, and expression, and for a refined connoisseurship and sureness of touch which were engendered by the long heritage of the past and the present promise of lasting peace.

Ara Pacis Augustae. Marble. Consecrated in 9 B.C. Lungotevere in Augusta, Rome

The "Altar of Peace," reconstructed from the surviving pieces, exactly symbolizes Augustus' policy. The outer sides of the altar enclosure are lavishly decorated with plant motifs and, above a meander pattern, with figures in relief; the longer sides feature a sacrificial procession of Romans with the imperial family, while the shorter ones, on either side of the entrances, show mythical and allegorical scenes illustrating the foundation and aims of the peace which Augustus had established.

The pronounced idealization of historical events extends even to the features of the persons portrayed here, and has thwarted attempts to establish their names.

Members of the Imperial Family. Detail from the south frieze of the *Ara Pacis*. Height of the figures, 61″

This motherly figure, surrounded by children, animals, and lavish vegetation, personifies the blessings of peace (see page 190).

Tellus. From the *Ara Pacis*

Augustus and Roma. Cameo of agate with a pale and a dark layer, $4^3/_8 \times 3^7/_8''$. c. 25 B.C. Kunsthistorisches Museum, Vienna

The figures are worked out in the light, transparent layer of the stone: they are Augustus, seated at ease upon a chair with Roma ostentatiously holding a shield before her. This may be the *clipeus virtutis* ("shield of virtue") awarded to Augustus in 27 B.C. Also the slight beard suggests that the work was produced at an early date. The association with the goddess personifying the city, as well as the double cornucopia, raises Augustus wholly above the human sphere. The mounting originates from the seventeenth century. The surviving part is probably only a fragment of a larger cameo.

The outlines were cut into the soft layer of stucco of the vaulted ceiling before the relief was applied. The flat elevation of the relief, the incision in the ground, and the color (no longer extant) produced, through the skillful use of perspective, an impression of three-dimensional space. Such landscapes with sacred edifices, votive pillars, and small idols were a favorite motif in wall paintings. According to the incised signature a certain Seleucus was the artist.

Sacred Landscape. Stucco relief from the bedchamber of a villa discovered in the garden of the Villa Farnesina, Rome. $15^3/_8 \times 24^3/_4''$. c. 20 B.C. Museo Nazionale Romano, Rome

Room in the "House of Livia." c. 25 B.C. Palatine Hill, Rome

This house, in which Augustus may have resided, is decorated in a manner also known to us from Pompeii. Above a socle the wall is divided up by columns, cornices, and niches resembling *aediculae* (small temples or shrines for statues), the intervening spaces being filled with paintings; the upper part contains glimpses of adjoining pillared halls, so that the wall itself seems to have dissolved away. In the large central panels are paintings (on the right: Io, Argus, Hermes; on the left: Polyphemus and Galatea) which give the illusion that one is looking out on the scenes depicted through "windows" in the wall. This is enhanced by the fact that there are actually sham "indoor" pictures on the upper part of the wall above the painted cornice.

Augustus with Drusus and Tiberius. Denarius. Silver, diameter ³/₄".
15–12 B.C. Private collection

On this silver coin, minted in Lugdunum (Lyon), Augustus is portrayed on the obverse in profile, whereas on the reverse he is depicted seated upon a high platform, receiving olive branches handed to him by Drusus and Tiberius. This scene relates to the victory in 15 B.C. over the Raeti and Vindelici.

The small Amor next to Augustus and the reliefs on the breastplate featuring Apollo, Artemis, Sol, Aurora, Tellus, and Caelus, as well as the Parthians returning the captured Roman standards (20 B.C.), make this portrait a symbol of Roman power, of the *Pax Romana.* The master of the world and prince of peace is a descendant of Venus who enjoys the special protection of the gods.

Augustus. Marble with traces of paint, height 80¹/₄". Shortly after 20 B.C. From the Villa of Livia, near Prima Porta, Rome. Vatican Museums, Rome

The death of Laocoön and his sons was depicted with plenty of movement but in very low relief by several artists working together; this restraint accords with the Augustan artistic ideal. Thus the efforts of Laocoön's elder son are suggested more by his posture than by any action on his part. The artists mentioned by Pliny are Agesander, Polydorus, and Athenodorus from Rhodes. They belonged to a family that produced generations of artists. Laocoön's death and the destruction of Troy are important events in the legendary prehistory of the foundation of Rome. Virgil describes them in detail in the *Aeneid* which he wrote at about the same time as this group was sculpted.

Laocoön. Marble, height 96″. c. 25 B.C. From the Esquiline Hill, Rome. Vatican Museums, Rome

This pointed amphora was produced by dipping the vessel into a white vitreous paste; the reliefs were cut from the white layer so formed. The three figures portrayed on each side of the vessel have not yet been satisfactorily interpreted, but the fact that they are juxtaposed in an almost motionless state must no doubt be seen in the context of some mythological event. One of the female figures on the other side can be identified —by a sea-dragon—as a sea-goddess. The base, which tapered to a point, is missing.

Allegory of Wealth. Silver plate with traces of gilding, diameter 11³/₄″. Beginning of first century A.D. From Aquileia. Kunsthistorisches Museum, Vienna

In the center of the dish Plutus is standing amidst personifications of fertility, while Zeus looks down from heaven. The *karpoi,* or fruits of the earth, which Plutus is receiving from the small children, must not fall haphazardly into the laps of the unjust; Zeus is watching to see that only the deserving are rewarded.

This slender figure, draped in an enveloping robe, is depicted in a graceful dancing movement. The statuette has been carefully worked from all sides, but in very low relief in conformity with the restraint of Augustan art.

Female Dancer. Marble, height 31¹/₂″. Beginning of first century A.D. From Fianello Sabino, Rome. Museo Nazionale Romano, Rome

The temple of Castor and Pollux (see page 94), vowed in 496 B.C. and dedicated in 484 B.C., was restored during the second century B.C. and later rebuilt by Tiberius. The Corinthian columns belong to this *peripteral* temple (having a row of columns on all sides), which had two porticoes with eight columns each, and eleven columns on either side. Tiberius dedicated the temple in his own name and that of his brother Drusus in A.D. 6.

Temple of the Dioscuri. Marble, height of podium 23', of columns 39'. A.D. 6. Forum Romanum, Rome

FIRST CENTURY A.D. (EARLY IMPERIAL PERIOD)

During the reigns of the Julio-Claudian and Flavian houses and during the reign of Trajan, there were "good" and "bad" emperors on the throne of Augustus. The territories of the Empire remained intact and were extended farther by successful wars under Trajan. For political reasons Augustus' immediate successors adhered to the artistic forms that had been binding during his era. Minor fluctuations of taste can be detected, such as further refinement under Tiberius, softer forms under Claudius and Nero, and, in general, perhaps a more pronounced tendency toward ostentatious display, though mostly in private life, for example, in mural decoration and in the minor arts. In public art, precisely because of its political importance, the precedents of the Augustan era were respected.

Nero's theatrical enthusiasm for everything Greek, his despotism, and also that of Domitian, favored a stronger revival of late Greek baroque art, whereas under Trajan, who in his campaigns seems to have had the image of Alexander the Great in his mind's eye, the art of that era was in fashion. He marked the conquests which brought the provinces of Dacia and Arabia into the Empire with extensive narrative scenes showing his deeds, and by building that splendid complex, the Forum of Trajan.

Cameo of Tiberius. Sardonyx with five layers, $12^{1}/_{4} \times 10^{1}/_{8}''$. Cabinet des Médailles, Bibliothèque Nationale, Paris

As was the case with Apulian vase paintings (see page 110), the three zones of the pictorial area correspond to three different spheres; from above those who are already numbered among the gods—including Augustus—look down upon events in the central register; in the lower one, there are prisoners to be seen. The action in the central register probably relates to Tiberius' dispatch of Germanicus to the eastern part of the Empire in A.D. 17; placed between the celestial and terrestrial spheres, it is left in a special "world of rulers" of its own.

Taste changed markedly after the earlier decorative illusionist painting. Indeed, architectonic elements are employed in this picture, but they are so flat and lacking in realism that the whole composition spreads across the wall like a two-dimensional ornament. This refined simplicity probably still accorded with late Augustan taste, but apparently did not become widely popular.

Wall decoration in the House of Lucretius Fronto, Pompeii. c. A.D. 20

The *Ara Pietatis* ("Altar ▶ of Fidelity"), a structure similar to the *Ara Pacis* (see page 190), was begun by Tiberius but consecrated by Claudius. The *flamen* in the procession wearing the typical sacerdotal cap with a tag may be Claudius. It is not known whereabouts in Rome the *Ara* once stood.

Procession. From the *Ara Pietatis Augustae.* Marble. A.D. 22–43. Villa Medici, Rome

Coastal Landscape. Detail. 23 x 27¹/₈″. Beginning of first century A.D. From Pompeii. Museo Nazionale, Naples

Together with the architectonic murals in Pompeii there often appear small paintings, either still lifes or landscapes. Those depicting the sea coast are of particular interest since they convey an idea of what the Bay of Naples looked like before A.D. 79. These small pictures are painted in a virtuoso manner reminiscent of the stucco reliefs (see page 194).

This slightly curved relief was part of the facing wall of a fountain; the lamb in its haste to reach its mother's milk has tipped over a pot from which the water of the fountain spurts forth. This idyll is symbolic of peace, as are the other reliefs of the wall, one of which, representing a lioness and her cub, is also well preserved. The delicacy, recalling that of a miniature, with which the marble has been worked is combined with a brush-like effect. The head of the sheep and parts of its legs have been reconstructed.

Landscape with Sheep. Marble, 37³/₈ × 31⁷/₈″. c. A.D. 50. Probably from Rome. Kunsthistorisches Museum, Vienna

For this representation the artist used a painting by Timanthes (fifth century B.C.) in which, according to ancient authors, ascending degrees of sorrow caused by Iphigenia's sacrifice are expressed in the faces of Calchas, Odysseus, Ajax, and Menelaus; Agamemnon veiled his face, and it is thus that he is portrayed in this relief. Scenery is confined to a single tree, and the figures are shown standing on the base line; at the time this was considered more classical than the arrangement of the figures around an altar with a certain spatial depth, as Timanthes had done combining them with a representation suggesting the temple complex.

Sacrifice of Iphigenia. Circular altar. Marble, height 25⅝″, diameter 16½″. Latter half of first century A.D. Signed by a certain Cleomenes. Uffizi Gallery, Florence

Mother and Son (Electra and Orestes). Marble, height 75⅝". C. A.D. 30. Museo Nazionale Romano, Rome

This group, in which a youth is shown gazing up at a matronly female, has been identified as Electra and Orestes, but the artist probably wanted merely to depict the intimate relationship between a young man and a motherly woman. He signed his work: "Menelaus, pupil of Stephanus, made this." There is a work signed by Stephanus with the statement that he was a pupil of Pasiteles, who lived about the time of Caesar. Menelaus made use of fourth-century prototypes for his group. The youth's right arm and the woman's left forearm have been reconstructed.

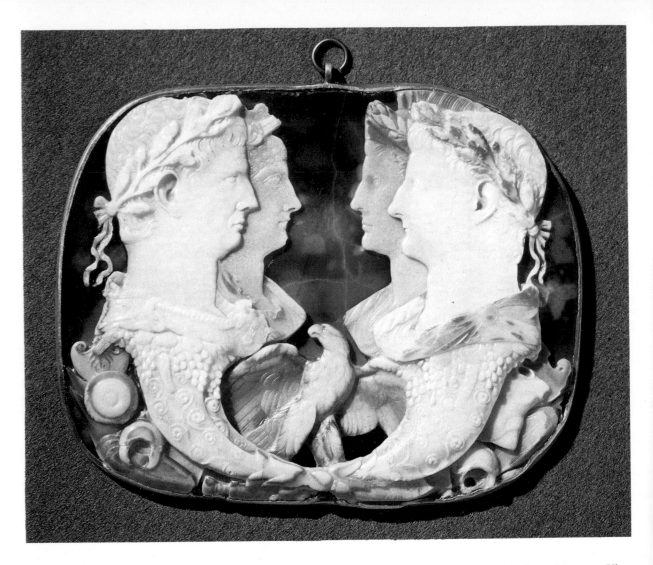

Cameo of Claudius. Sardonyx with several white and brown layers, 4³/₄ x 6″. c. A.D. 48. Kunsthistorisches Museum, Vienna

The busts of Claudius, Agrippina the Younger, Germanicus, and Agrippina the Elder are supported by cornucopias crossed over weapons, symbolizing a prosperous future. This cameo was probably made for Claudius' marriage to Agrippina, whose parents appear on the right; Germanicus was also the Emperor's brother. In this work the ancient art of cameo engraving reaches its final climax.

From a fairly long frieze there survive the figures of Claudius, Germanicus, Antonia, and Augustus shown here; to the left is a fragment of a seated woman (Agrippina the Younger?); further figures to the right may have been Livia, Tiberius, and Drusus. The members of the imperial dynasty are portrayed as a row of statues. Such groups were erected throughout the Empire by Claudius to show that he was the legitimate ruler. From the same monument we have another fragment showing a sacrificial procession.

The Julio-Claudian Family. Marble. c. A.D. 50. Museo Nazionale, Ravenna

Against a red ground the Nereid glides past, mounted on a sea horse. This ancient motif of a happy and care-free existence (see pages 161 ff.) is well suited to these murals which served as a background to scenes of merrymaking.

Nereid Riding a Sea Horse. 18⅞ x 29⅞″. c. A.D. 65. From Stabiae. Museo Nazionale, Naples

Theater at Taormina. Diameter 357′ 6″, of orchestra 115′. Latter half of first century A.D.

This Greek theater, probably built during the third century B.C., was adapted to changed requirements during the early Imperial period. Thenceforth the auditorium formed a complete semicircle directly adjoining the proscenium; this had a magnificent facade (*scaenae frons*) embellished with columns, niches, and statues. The theater at Taormina is situated on a rocky eminence from which one can obtain commanding views of the sea and Mount Etna.

The House of the Vettii was decorated in accordance with the taste of the era between the earthquake of A.D. 62 and the final destruction of the city by the eruption of Vesuvius in A.D. 79. The elegance of the earlier decoration (page 204) has given way to illusionist architectural painting which attempts to dissolve the walls away (see pages 183, 195)—just as had been done before as early as the end of the first century B.C. The remaining wall spaces were occupied by copies of famous "classical" Greek paintings.

Galba Addressing His Soldiers (A.D. 68–69). Sesterce, struck posthumously under Vespasian. Bronze, diameter 1³/₈″. Ashmolean Museum, Oxford

Galba is shown standing on a podium, placed obliquely, with a companion behind him; he is addressing some soldiers who are standing in an irregular group on the ground before him with weapons and banners towering above them. The inscription ADLOCUTIO ("address") in the lower segment of the coin identifies this formal occasion. This little coin no doubt reproduces a painting designed to exemplify the close relationship between the Emperor and his army.

Triumphal Procession of Titus. Relief on the Arch of Titus. Marble, 94¹/₂ × 152″. A.D. 80–90. Forum Romanum, Rome

The two reliefs in the passageway of this monument, erected after Titus' death (A.D. 81), depict scenes from the triumph which Titus and his father, Vespasian, held in A.D. 71 to commemorate the victory in Palestine. On one side is Titus in the triumphal chariot, on the other the spoils being carried from the Temple in Jerusalem, including the seven-branched candelabrum, the table for the shewbread, and the trumpets. The two badly preserved figures in the foreground, on the left-hand border and a little to the right of the center, may be identified as Domitian and Vespasian.

The walls of the inner court of this house are decorated with mosaics. On either side of this one, there are canthari with sprouting tendrils, landscapes with animals chasing one another, and hanging garlands; the two sea-gods are represented in the center here. Enclosed within broad ornamental bands and a border of sea-shells, they stand like statues side by side under a fan-shaped canopy. Mosaic art, originally designed to embellish floors, was extended to walls as well and reached a new peak early in the Christian era.

Poseidon and Amphitrite. Mosaic in the inner court of the Casa del Mosaico di Nettuno e di Anfitrite ("House of the Mosaic of Neptune and Amphitrite"), Herculaneum. c. A.D. 70

The Flavian amphitheater, which obtained its popular name from Nero's colossus nearby, was begun by Vespasian in a basin-shaped valley between the Esquiline and the Caelian Hills. It was completed by Titus, who added the fourth story. The building, designed for popular amusements, was consecrated with games that lasted for a hundred days. For the eighty external arcaded openings the architect used the Tuscan, Ionic, and Corinthian orders which are superimposed one above the other. This sequence was an important model for Renaissance architecture, as were the Corinthian pilasters of the fourth story.

Colosseum. Travertine, c. 613 x 508'. Consecrated in A.D. 80. Rome

Heracles. Green schist, height 11' 8". End of first century A.D. From the Palatine, Rome. Museo Nazionale di Antichità, Parma

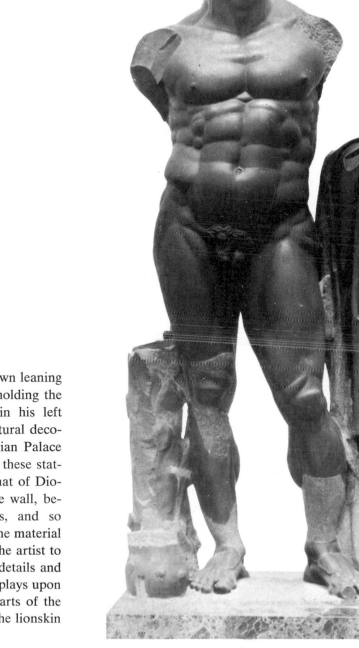

This statue of Heracles, shown leaning upon a club and probably holding the apples of the Hesperides in his left hand, was part of the sculptural decoration of a hall in the Flavian Palace on the Palatine. Another of these statues which has survived is that of Dionysus. They stood along the wall, between polychrome columns, and so formed part of the decor. The material used, green schist, enabled the artist to be extremely precise in the details and to bring out the light which plays upon the vast curving surfaces. Parts of the legs and the block beneath the lionskin have been restored.

Cleobis and Biton. Altar. Marble, height 29½″. Toward the end of the first century A.D. From Via Cassia, Rome. Museo Nazionale Romano, Rome

This altar was decorated on all four sides by reliefs (Dionysus, Artemis, Actaeon, and a stag in a rocky landscape). The best preserved of them shows the two brothers Cleobis and Biton drawing the chariot of their mother Cydippe, the priestess of Hera at Argos. Herodotus (I, 31) relates the story and how the brothers were rewarded for their deed. Two statues at Delphi perpetuated their memory. To the Romans they were an example of *Pietas* ("dutiful conduct").

The bearded man carrying a scepter in his hand personifies the Roman Senate and the youth behind him the Roman people. They are welcoming the decision of the Emperor Nerva, despite his sixty-five years, to follow Mars and Victoria, who is shown flying on ahead. Minerva stands beside him. Gods, personified concepts, and real figures are mingled in this scene based on a particular historical event. ▶

The Roman Senate, Populace, and Soldiers. Marble, height 80¾″. A.D. 96–98. Found below the Cancelleria, Rome. Vatican Museums, Rome

The forum dedicated by Nerva in A.D. 97 was surrounded by a frieze in relief about 1300 feet long, which followed the projections of the architrave above the columns. It related legends and events centering upon Minerva. Surviving parts depict the contest between Athena and Arachne, who when defeated was transformed into a spider, and a ceremony of guild members and artisans in honor of their tutelary goddess. With their almost rigid matter-of-factness these decorative reliefs, which could only be seen from a considerable distance, bear a strong resemblance to those of the Nerva monument (see below).

SECOND CENTURY A.D. (MIDDLE IMPERIAL PERIOD)

The "simple soldier" Trajan, who adhered to ancient Italic custom in letting his hair fall naturally across his brow, differed in outward appearance from his adopted son, Hadrian, who wore his hair in curls and had a beard—a style which had been out of fashion in Italy since the time of Alexander the Great and was still worn only by the philosophers. Hadrian's philhellenism was not entirely devoid of romantic traits. It took the form of extensive journeyings in the East and the building there of numerous splendid edifices for government or public use. This led to a new vogue for classicism. Noble Romans followed the Emperor's example by visiting the ancient cultural sites in Greece, using the writings of Pausanias as a guide. A widespread desire arose to own at least copies of famous Greek works and the output of such copies rose accordingly. The influence of Augustan artistic precedents faded in the face of these new impulses derived directly from Greece, and it is this source that now inspired almost every genre of art, especially that of reliefs on sarcophagi. At the moment when Roman power was at its height, there was thus a renewed movement toward the assimilation of Greek art, and the hitherto scarcely known custom of burying the dead in marble sarcophagi, and in particular of decorating them with scenes taken from Greek myth or from life, suddenly spread. This almost suggests that the feeling that they had now reached the climax of their achievements and were henceforth on the decline had drained the Romans of their vitality. A yearning for the better and more beautiful life of the Hereafter is often reflected in the scenes on the sarcophagi.

Hadrian's classicist trends were in the main continued by his successors, even though Antoninus Pius tried to steer a course nearer to the ideals of ancient Roman virtue, on which Rome's greatness had been founded.

The technique of marble sculpture reached an unsurpassed height. Separate strands of hair were reproduced by ingenious drilling, and the contrast of the rough hair surface was used to set off the highly polished skin. The custom was also begun of indicating the glance of the eye by light and shade, created by hollowing out the pupil to a certain depth, instead of by painting as before. This "impressionistic" device was but one more expression of an incipient shift away from bodily realism in sculpture and toward the suggestion of effects by optical means, a trend which was to become ever stronger.

Trajan's Column. Marble, height of relief at bottom 35³/₈″, at top 49¹/₄″. Consecrated on May 18, A.D. 113. Forum Trajani, Rome

This column, which was formerly crowned by a statue of the Emperor, has a spiral band of reliefs round its shaft. The thirty-six spirals have about 2,500 figures and tell of Trajan's wars against the Dacians (A.D. 101–2 and 105–7).

Hitherto generals' military successes had only been recorded in this way in paintings; the idea of commemorating them in relief on a column may have originated with Apollodorus of Damascus, the architect of Trajan's Forum. In the base of the column Trajan's ashes were interred in A.D. 117.

The battle reliefs used by Constantine in his triumphal arch probably belonged originally to the decoration of Trajan's Forum, finished in A.D. 113. There they formed a much longer sequence than is suggested by the parts on Constantine's Arch and other extant fragments. Battle scenes alternate with those of an allegorical character. With its closely packed figures in several layers of relief, the style is related to that of Flavian art.

Trajan's Battle with the Dacians. Marble, height 9′ 9³/₈″. Beginning of second century A.D. On the Arch of Constantine, Rome

Trajan's Arch. Marble. A.D. 114–17. Beneventum (Benevento)

This arch commemorates the completion of the road between Beneventum and Brundisium (A.D. 114) and is particularly lavishly decorated with fourteen huge reliefs. The side facing the city portrays the Emperor's relations with Rome, and the other his relations with the provinces and foreign powers. Here, too, the style reveals a close connection with Flavian art (see page 216), but the restraining influence still exerted by the Nerva reliefs cannot be overlooked.

Hadrian as a Hunter. Marble, diameter 92⅞″. A.D.
130–38. Arch of Constantine (see page 250), Rome

Pantheon. Height 142′, diameter of cupola 142′. ▶
After A.D. 126. Piazza della Rotonda, Rome

◄ The eight reliefs on the *tondi* (round plaques) which Constantine incorporated into his arch were probably designed to be placed in pairs on a tetrapylon, a monument with four gateways, on which Hadrian immortalized his successes as a huntsman. Each hunting scene is accompanied by its appropriate sacrifice; two reliefs describe the departure for the hunt and the sacrifice performed on returning. Hadrian's passion for the chase is also commemorated in coins struck with the inscription VIRTUTI AUGUSTI ("to the courage of Augustus").

The Pantheon, erected by Agrippa in A.D. 23, was completely rebuilt by Hadrian after it had twice been destroyed by fire; the inscription, however, only mentions Agrippa: M. AGRIPPA L. F. COS TERTIUM FECIT ("Marcus Agrippa, son of Lucius, built [it] when consul for the third time"). The cupola, of which the height is equal to the diameter, has at its crown a circular opening 29′ 6″ wide; it is the most impressive interior to have survived from antiquity. The portico (108′ 3″ x 42′ 8″) has sixteen monolithic granite columns which form a double colonnade. The area of the pediment was probably once decorated with a huge bronze relief.

Hadrian's Villa near ▶ Tibur (Tivoli). A.D. 120–30

Consecratio ("Apo-theosis") of Sabina. Marble, height 8′ 5″. Shortly after A.D. 136. From the Arco di Portogallo ("Arch of Portugal"), Rome. Palazzo dei Conservatori, Rome

The Empress Sabina is shown being carried up to heaven by the winged Aeternitas ("Eternity") after her death in A.D. 136. This deification is witnessed by Hadrian, by the adopted Antoninus Pius behind him, and by Campus Martius (the personification of the Field of Mars), reclining on the floor to the left.

The style of this relief is characteristic of the classicism of Hadrian's reign, which could develop more fully on a semiallegorical theme as here, than in the pendant where Hadrian is shown delivering a eulogy for Sabina. The hands and much of Hadrian's head, the head of Antoninus Pius, the forearms of Aeternitas, and other parts have been made good since Roman times.

After his journeys to all the provinces of the Empire, Hadrian built in gentle hilly country near Tivoli a huge villa which was to reflect the whole Roman world in miniature. During the final period of construction there arose this magnificent complex, situated in a valley artificially cut into the hill, with a reservoir some 330 feet long, lined with columns and numerous statues. The complex ended in a *triclinium* (dining room) in a

monumental grotto. There were statues of crocodiles and other reminders of Egypt—such as the canal which led from Alexandria to the suburb of Canopus, where the Temple of Serapis stood. The statue of the Amazon is a copy of the original by Phidias.

Temple of Faustina. After A.D. 141. Forum Romanum, Rome

This temple, converted into a church (San Lorenzo in Miranda) during the eleventh century, was built in memory of Faustina; when Antoninus Pius died twenty years later (A.D. 161) it became a place of emperor-worship. The inscription DIVO ANTONINO ET DIVAE FAUSTINAE EX S.C. ("to the deified Antoninus and the deified Faustina by decree of the Senate") shows distinctly that Antoninus' name was added later. The temple stands upon a high podium and has at the front six monolithic columns of Cipollino marble, with two more on either side. The *cella,* of peperino, is embellished with a marble frieze featuring pairs of griffins placed antithetically.

The base of the Templum Divi Hadriani (temple of the deified Hadrian), erected by Hadrian's successor Antoninus Pius, bore reliefs representing weapons and personifications of the Roman provinces. Sixteen of the twenty provinces have survived; they are no longer humble subjects, as on Augustus' breastplate (see page 197), but representatives of imperial territories who stand erect with their own dignity. They were modeled on classical statues.

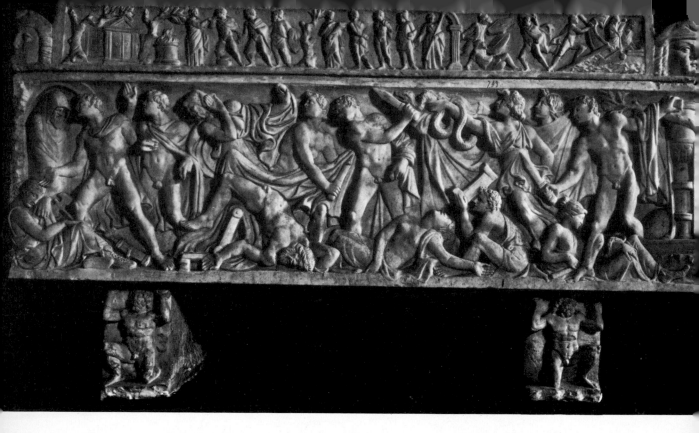

The Orestes Sarcophagus. Marble, 26 x 84⁵/₈ x 31¹/₂″. Mid-second century A.D. From Rome. Museo Profano, Lateran, Rome

The tale of the death of Aegisthus and Clytemnestra at the hand of Orestes, who had vowed to avenge his murdered father, is narrated in individual episodes up to the point where the matricide seeks Apollo's protection at Delphi from persecution by the Furies. The artist probably took as his model a painting by the classical artist Theorus. On the sides are depicted the Furies and the shades of Aegisthus and Clytemnestra. The frieze on the lid portrays Orestes' vicissitudes in Tauris.

The only equestrian statue of the innumerable ones that existed in antiquity to have survived is that of Marcus Aurelius, which Michelangelo made the center of the piazza on the Capitol. The Emperor, in soldier's garb, is greeting his subjects. According to the *Mirabilia urbis* ("Marvels of Rome"), under the horse's hoof there was a "small king," i.e., a subject potentate. This figure simultaneously served to support the weight of the statue; in its absence the statue today is perceptibly overbalanced to the right. It is not known where the statue originally stood, but it was certainly not on top of a triumphal arch.

Marcus Aurelius Distributing Money. Marble, height 9′ 10″, width 76³/₄″. After A.D. 176. From the attic on the north side of Constantine's Arch, Rome (see page 250)

This relief, which once adorned a triumphal arch of Marcus Aurelius, represents a *congiarium* or distribution of money to the Roman people on the occasion of the victory over the Marcomanni. In two zones, one above the other, are typical representatives of the people and the Emperor upon a podium with his attendants. The facade of columns in the background could be the Temple of Faustina (see page 230). The Emperor's head has been restored.

The portrait-like features of Mars and Venus indicate that here an imperial couple have had themselves depicted in this form—probably the young Commodus and Crispina (d. A.D. 187). Emperors and empresses were already being deified in this way during their lifetime, in accord with an idea which had been current since the age of Alexander the Great and had struck root in Rome during the time of Caesar.

Commodus and Crispina (?) as Mars and Venus. Marble, height 87¾". A.D. 178–80. From Ostia. Museo Nazionale Romano, Rome

Marcus Aurelius' Column. Marble, height (including statue) 137' 10", height of spiral relief 51⅝". A.D. 176–93. Piazza Colonna, Rome

This column commemorates Marcus Aurelius' victory over the Sarmatians and Marcomanni in A.D. 176. The band of reliefs winding round the column in twenty-four spirals describes the events of the war. The artist has clearly taken Trajan's Column (see page 223) as his model, but has concentrated more heavily upon essentials and enlarged the scale of the figures, so that the viewer can make out as much as possible from below. The column is freestanding, whereas that of Trajan stood in the court of a multistoried library. When the Emperor Marcus Aurelius died (A.D. 180), the column was still unfinished and served as a funerary monument for him. Even by A.D. 193 it was still not complete.

This marine *thiasus* (dance in honor of Bacchus) ▶ once again symbolizes man's expectations of life in the Hereafter. On sarcophagi, as in various other works, the idea is conveyed in the allegory of the long journey of the deceased across the waves to Elysium.

Nereid Riding a Sea Centaur. Detail from a sarcophagus. Marble, height of Nereid 26³/₈″. End of second century A.D. Museo Nazionale Romano, Rome

Dionysus and Ariadne on Naxos. Sarcophagus. Height 35⁷/₈″. End of second century A.D. Vatican Museums, Rome

Dionysus' discovery of Ariadne, deserted by Theseus, serves as an inspiration for this artist to depict the Dionysian thiasus in a large number of individual scenes. That of the female centaur, resting together with her small son after having drawn the god's chariot, has a particular idyllic charm. It also recalls the *Centaur Family* of Zeuxis (fifth century B.C.). In other respects, too, it is apparent that the artist was familiar with all the rich treasures of ancient art. The torsos of Dionysus and the two maenads behind him have been reconstructed.

THIRD AND EARLY FOURTH CENTURY A.D. (LATE IMPERIAL PERIOD)

This was an age of change: Caracalla bestowed Roman citizenship upon all free men dwelling within the Empire (A.D. 212), bloody conflicts broke out between rival contenders for the imperial throne, Rome's enemies in the north and east grew more powerful so that Aurelian found it necessary to have the city walled round, the Christians were being persecuted, and Rome's internal authority seemed on the verge of collapse.

It is only too understandable how people at imperial coronations in these days conjured up an idealized picture of the reigns of Augustus and Trajan, now that those happy eras were receding ever further into the past. That the Roman Empire survived for so long is as astonishing as the stubborn persistence of artistic activity, for the reliefs on the sarcophagi show no noticeable signs of decline. In cultural as in political life there were still periods of "renaissance" within this era, i.e., efforts to return to a mood of peace and contemplation through the evocation of the good old days; but now these revivals were of shorter duration.

The efforts of Diocletian, in collaboration with his co-ruler Maximianus Herculius (Maximian), to achieve a new political stability meant that all possible aids, including art, were pressed into service of this goal. The portraits of the two Emperors, and of both the "Caesars" they designated as their heirs, are political documents and proclaim their equality and unity in every feature. There was no longer any interest in individuality or beauty, for the real purpose of art was now political testament.

Constantine, who emerged as victor from the conflicts that followed the breakdown of this carefully worked out system of succession, encouraged the people to look back to Augustus and the "good" emperors, with whose images in relief he adorned his triumphal arch. But Constantine also inaugurates a new era. The

Dionysus and Ariadne on Naxos. See facing page

court ceremonial borrowed from the East, which conferred on the absolute ruler an almost celestial status, found a counterpart in an art which, in apparent emulation of ancient oriental models, emphasized the distance between him and lowly mortals. This is the clearest indication of what a gulf had opened up between now and the humanity of the age of an Alexander or an Augustus. It is the end of an attitude toward the world that was secular and by and large respectful of the freedom of the individual. The new outlook that replaced it fused the secular and the divine into an indivisible unity. Art had a new task to fulfill in the scheme of things in a world wholly given over to the service of the lord of all in heaven and earth.

Phaedra. Sarcophagus. Height 46¹/₈″, length of front 89³/₄″, of ends 43¹/₄″ and 34⁵/₈″. c. A.D. 200. Santa Nicola, Agrigento

Arch of Septimius Severus. Marble. A.D. 203. Forum Romanum, Rome

On top of this arch was a six-horse chariot, in which stood Severus and his two sons, Caracalla and Geta. The arch is designed grandly, with a huge relief over each of the side archways retelling the Emperor's deeds of war in the East. In each panel two different events are presented one above the other; although this does not conform to the greatest optical realism, it nevertheless makes for ease of narration.

◀ The four sides of this sarcophagus depict the ensnarement of Phaedra in a love affair with her stepson, Hippolytus, and his death instigated by her denunciation of him in her disappointment. On the front of the sarcophagus Hippolytus is seen amidst his hunting companions, looking at the letter from Phaedra; on the rear he is hunting boar on horseback. On one end (opposite) is the lovesick Phaedra, surrounded by her attendants, and on the other is Hippolytus falling to his death. After Johann Hermann von Riedesel had admired and correctly interpreted the sarcophagus in 1767, Goethe was moved to visit it on his Sicilian journey.

241

Sarcophagus with battle scene. Marble. Third century A.D. From Via Tiburtina, Rome. Museo Nazionale Romano, Rome ▶

The man in the center, joining hands in marriage with his bride, must have been an official of high rank, since among those present is the personification of the Roman Senate. The figures of Ceres, Annona, Africa, and Portus Romae indicate that he looked after the corn supply, i.e., was *Praefectus Annonae* (chief official for food). The woman behind the couple is Concordia. On the ridge above the relief are a few traces of explanatory inscriptions. The figures stand out against a curtain suspended behind them and formerly painted a golden yellow. The other sides of the sarcophagus are plain.

Sarcophagus with wedding scene. Marble, with traces of painting, height 34¼", length 82¼". c. A.D. 275. From Rome (near Porta Latina). Museo Nazionale Romano, Rome

Amid the confusion of battle the commander in chief is charging the barbarians. His face was to have been worked as a portrait, but this was not done. The scene is entirely filled with warriors in turmoil, some victorious, some vanquished, and is framed at the sides by trophies and prisoners. The lid of the sarcophagus has a border featuring the general's wedding and an act of *clementia* (mercy) on his part.

Aurelian as a Builder of Rome's City Wall. Clay, 11³/₈ × 34⁵/₈". c. A.D. 275. From Via Cassia, Rome. Museo Nazionale Romano, Rome

The kneeling goddess Roma is expressing her thanks to the Emperor Aurelian for delivering her from the barbarian threat and for the protection which his building of the city wall has afforded her. In A.D. 271 the Emperor succeeded at the last moment in defeating the invading Germanic tribes and preventing the fall of Rome. The ancient walls had long since ceased to afford any protection to the city, which had grown tremendously. The new ring wall, of which much still remains today, is the Emperor's lasting achievement and a monument to his foresight. The trophies behind him recall his victory; to the right and left there are laborers using hoists in the building of the gates. It is more than likely that the completion of the wall was commemorated in a huge painting, of which such clay reliefs as this were just reproductions. A second one has also survived. The brickkilns played the greatest part in the supply of materials for the construction of the wall, which measured some twelve miles in length. This relief decorated one of the large bricks.

This monument once consisted of five tall columns with statues of Jupiter, the two Emperors Diocletian and Maximian, and the two Caesars Galerius and Constantius Chlorus. The base of one of these statues is all that has survived. It features Victories holding a shield which reads CAESARUM DECENNALIA FELICITER ("the ten-year festival of the Caesars was successful"). The monument commemorates the tenth anniversary of this constitutional system which was intended to ensure continuity of government, and also the twentieth year of the two Emperors' reign. The other three sides of the base depict a sacrifice to Mars: Constantius Chlorus, in the presence of the god and Roma, is making the preliminary sacrifice with a procession of citizens and soldiers approaching from the adjoining right-hand side and a number of sacrificial animals —a bull, a sheep, and a pig—being brought up from the opposite side.

Base of a monument to the Tetrarchs. Marble, height of relief 41³/₄", width 70⁷/₈". A.D. 303. Forum Romanum, Rome

This imperial villa is located in a picturesque valley and was probably used on hunting expeditions. This is indicated by extensive scenes of the chase in the floor mosaic which covers approximately 4,200 square yards and is thus the largest mosaic area of antiquity. The old man leaning upon a staff and a bodyguard has been tentatively identified as Maximian, especially since he is wearing a diadem. But the idea of people treading upon an image of the Emperor is of course foreign to such an identification.

These two Emperors and Caesars have been taken from a column which stood in Constantinople. One of the missing feet has recently been discovered in Istanbul. By representing them in this form, it was intended to demonstrate that the rulers were united as a guarantee to the public of the continuing welfare of the Roman Empire. On account of its purple color, porphyry was reserved for imperial use. The portraits of the Emperors and Caesars are so standardized, thereby further emphasizing their unity, that it is impossible to identify them individually.

Galerius Engaged in Battle.
From the Arch of Galerius,
Salonika. Marble, overall
length of frieze 12′ 5⅝″.
A.D. 297–305

This tetrapylon is covered throughout with reliefs depicting Galerius' deeds during his campaign against the Parthians in A.D. 297. The various friezes are separated by broad ornamental bands. Above the triumphant Galerius soars the eagle of Jupiter with the victor's laurels. Only two of the four piers of the arch, which formed the entrance to a spacious palace precinct, have survived.

Basilica of Constantine. Height of aisles 80′ 4″, original height of central nave 114′ 10″, width 82′, length 196′ 10″. A.D. 307–13. Forum Romanum, Rome

This building, begun by Maxentius, was completed by Constantine who changed the entrance round to the Forum side. The huge brick structure, covering an area of over 7,000 square yards, was decorated with marble columns and costly wall paneling; the apse in the center of the northern aisle was designed for use by the reigning emperor and his retinue. The central nave of the vaulting, of which only the lowest parts have been preserved, was only ten feet lower than the nave of Cologne Cathedral.

Arch of Constantine. Marble. A.D. 313–15. Near the
Colosseum, Rome

Youth of Achilles. Silver plate, diameter 20⁷/₈″. c. A.D. 350. ▶
From Augst. Museum, Augst

On this triumphal arch, erected after the Battle at the Milvian Bridge, only one of the small relief friezes
deals with this decisive event. The rest of the decoration was almost entirely borrowed from other ancient
monuments, probably for two reasons: to complete the monument quickly and also to herald the return of
good government—for all these reliefs originate from the reigns of "good" emperors: Trajan (see page 224),
Hadrian (see page 226), and Marcus Aurelius (see page 234). From the reign of Constantine himself are the
impressive *tondi* on the narrow sides representing the rising Sol and the setting Moon-goddess.

The border of this octagonal dish represents in great detail the birth of Achilles, his education by the centaur Chiron, and his life among the daughters of Lycomedes. The medallion in the center concludes the portrayal of his youth: through Odysseus' cunning Achilles is discovered among the maidens. Another silver plate probably described the hero's later vicissitudes in a similar fashion.

Muse. Marble, height 73⅝″. Fourth century A.D. Uffizi Gallery, Florence

This Muse, identifiable by the *cithara* (Greek lyre-like instrument with wooden sounding board) as Erato, is the work of a certain Atticianes from Aphrodisias, as the Latin signature on the base indicates. The statue is the last one in antiquity to be signed and adheres closely to classical tradition in regard to theme and motif at a time when Christianity had long been setting the fashion.

800 B.C.	(814 Foundation of Carthage)	From 1000 Villanovan culture	Geometric art
	753 Foundation of Rome 750–510 Kings in Rome	Italic Geometric pottery	Homer 776 First records of Olympic Games
	734 Foundation of Syracuse		745–727 Reign of Tiglath-pileser III in Assyria
	710 Foundation of Croton		722 End of Israelite state 714 Assyria defeats Urartu
700	708 Foundation of Tarentum (Taranto)		
700 B.C.		Oriental art imported	Early archaic art
	688 Foundation of Gela	Tomba Bernardini	Hesiod Tyrants
	675 Foundation of Rhegium (Reggio)	Pietrera sculptures	680–652 Gyges King of Lydia
	625(?) Foundation of Selinus (Selinunte)	Early Corinthian pottery imported	620 Draco
	615 Tarquinian kings in Rome	Local imitations	
600			
600 B.C.		Bucchero pottery *Centaur* from Vulci	594 Solon Sappho. Alcaeus
	585 Foundation of Acragas (Agrigento)	*Goddess* from Vulci	585 Thales 586 Jerusalem destroyed by Nebuchadnezzar
	570–534 Phalaris	Corinthian pottery imported Treasury at Foce del Sele Chariot from Monteleone South Temple at Paestum Attic pottery imported	561–528 Pisistratus 560–546 Croesus
	540 Xenophanes settles in Elea Parmenides	Caeretan hydriae	534 Thespis 538–522 Polycrates
	535 Battle off Alalia	Temple C at Selinus Terra-cotta sarcophagus from Caere (Cerveteri)	Buddha. Confucius
	525 Pythagoras	Tomba del Barone Terra-cotta statue from Veii Vulca in Rome	520–515 Building of temple at Jerusalem
	511 Destruction of Sybaris 510 Tarquins expelled from Rome		510 Hippias, son of Pisistratus, expelled from Athens
500			
500 B.C.	496 Battle of Lake Regillus 494–476 Anaxilas of Rhegium 485 Gelon 480 Carthaginians defeated at Himera	Forum Romanum rebuilt Temple of Jupiter on the Capitol dedicated 493 Temple of Ceres in Rome 484 Temple of the Dioscuri in Rome	Temple of Aphaea on Aegina 490 Battle of Marathon 480 Battle of Salamis Pericles
	474 Hiero defeats Etruscans at Cumae 451 Law of XII Tables	Capitoline *She-Wolf* Ludovisi throne Temple of Hera at Paestum	Temple of Zeus at Olympia Pythagoras. Myron Aeschylus Parthenon
	443 Foundation of Thurii	Temple E at Selinus Early Italiote vases	Phidias. Polycletus
	420 Fall of Cumae 412 Athenians defeated off Syracuse 409 Fall of Himera and Selinus 405 Fall of Acragas Siege of Veii	431 Temple of Apollo in Rome Temple at Segesta Temple F at Acragas	Sophocles Temple of Apollo at Bassae Euripides Sicilian expedition Socrates
	405 Dionysius I of Syracuse Pompeii under Samnite domination		
400			

400 B.C.	395 Romans conquer Veii		399 Death of Socrates
	387 Gauls in Rome Beginning of Roman expansion in Etruria	380 Servian Wall *Chimaera* of Arezzo	Praxiteles
	367 Death of Dionysius I Plato in Sicily	Amazon sarcophagus (Florence) Sarcophagus (Boston) Apulian, Lucanian, Campanian pottery	Mausoleum of Halicarnassus Scopas
	343–341 First Samnite War	Lysippus in Tarentum	336–323 Alexander Leochares, Lysippus
	326–304 Second Samnite War		322 Death of Demosthenes and Aristotle
		312 Via Appia. Aqua Appia Novius Plautius 304 Fabius Pictor, Temple of Salus	
300			
300 B.C.	291 Capitulation of Samnites 287 End of civil wars 283 Battle of Lake Vadimo 282–272 War with Pyrrhus 270 Italy under Roman domination	François Tomb Scipio sarcophagus Etruscan sarcophagi	282 Foundation of kingdom of Pergamon 280 Celts invade Greece and Asia Minor 250 Foundation of Parthian kingdom
	264–241 First Punic War	269 Beginning of Roman silver coinage	241–197 Attalus I
	222 Gauls defeated at Battle of Clastidium 218–201 Second Punic War 212 Syracuse conquered Death of Archimedes 202 Victory at Zama	Gnathian pottery *Ram* of Syracuse 211 Captured works of art exhibited by Marcellus Calene relief ware	230 Greeks defeated on River Caicus 222–187 Antiochus the Great
200	200 Naevius, *Bellum Punicum*	Temple on Lake Argentino	*Septuaginta*
200 B.C.	Scipio 189 Eumenes in Rome 188 Rome dominates the eastern Mediterranean	Temple of Magna Mater in Rome Porta Marzia, Perugia Tomba del Tifone Memorial to Scipio's victory(?)	197 Flamininus wins victory at Cynoscephalae 197–159 Eumenes II Pergamon altar 190 Victory at Magnesia *Eagle* cameo
	184 Death of Plautus Cato the Censor 167 Polybius in Rome 159 Death of Terence 146 Carthage and Corinth destroyed	179 Basilicas in Forum Many works of art looted in the East are brought to Rome	*Telephus* painting discovered 168 Victory of Aemilius Paulus in Battle of Pydna 167 Rebellion of Maccabees *Venus de Milo*
	133 Beginning of Roman civil wars. Gracchi 101 Marius defeats Cimbri near Vercellae	Tufa period in Pompeii Incrustation style	138–133 Attalus III 133 Rome inherits Pergamon
100			
100 B.C.	91–88 Social War 88 Italian enfranchisement 86 Death of Marius 82–78 Sulla dictator 80 Pompeii a Roman colony 66 Pompey 73–71 Verres in Sicily 63 Catiline conspiracy 58–51 Caesar conquers Gaul 44 Assassination of Caesar 43 Assassination of Cicero Birth of Ovid 31 Victory at Actium 19 Death of Virgil	Pasiteles Arcesilaus Architectural style in Pompeii Arretine *terra sigillata* *Laocoön* *Augustus* of Prima Porta 9 *Ara Pacis Augustae*	Mithridates VI of Pontus 64 Syria and Pontus Roman provinces 53 Loss of banners to the Parthians 47–30 Cleopatra 30 Egypt becomes Roman 20 Parthians return banners Birth of Christ

A.D. 1	9 Battle of Teutoburg Forest		
	14 Death of Augustus	Ornamental style in Pompeii	
	14–37 Tiberius	17 Cameo of Tiberius	
	17 Death of Ovid		
	37–41 Caligula		
	41–54 Claudius	48 Cameo of Claudius	50 St. Paul in Corinth
	Works on Etruscan history		
	54–68 Nero		
	64 Burning of Rome		66–68 Nero in Greece
	Lucan, Seneca		
	68/69 Galba, Otho, Vitellius	Illusionist style in Pompeii	70 Jerusalem captured
	69–79 Vespasian		
	79–81 Titus		
	79 Destruction of Pompeii,	80 Colosseum	
	death of Pliny		
	81–96 Domitian	80–90 Arch of Titus	
	96–98 Nerva		
100		Forum Romanum	
A.D. 100	98–117 Trajan		
	101–7 Dacian Wars	113 Trajan's Forum and Column	
	117–38 Hadrian	Pantheon. Castel S. Angelo	114–17 Parthian War
	120 Death of Tacitus	120–30 Hadrian's villa at Tivoli	120 Death of Plutarch
	138–61 Antoninus Pius		132–35 Bar-Cocheba rebellion
	161–80 Marcus Aurelius	Equestrian statue on the Capitol	
	167–80 Marcomannic War	176–93 Marcus Aurelius' Column	176 Pausanias, *Periegesis of*
	180–92 Commodus		*Greece*
	193 Pertinax, Pescennius Niger,		180 Death of Lucian
	Clodius Albinus		
200	193–211 Septimius Severus		195–99 Parthian Wars
A.D. 200	211–17 Caracalla	203 Arch of Septimius Severus	
	212 All inhabitants of the	200–30 Baths in Rome	227 Sassanian empire founded by
	empire made Roman citizens		Ardashir I
	218–22 Elagabalus		
	222–35 Alexander Severus		
	235–84 Soldier emperors		
	248 Millennial celebrations		260 Valerian taken prisoner by
	in Rome		Shapur I
	253–68 Gallienus		267–72 Zenobia Queen of
	205–70 Plotinus, Neoplatonism		Palmyra
	260 Destruction of the *limes*	City walls in Rome	268 Heruli invade Greece
	270–75 Aurelian	299 Baths of Diocletian	Porphyry statues
300	284–305 Diocletian's tetrarchy	Villa, Piazza Armerina	297–305 Arch of Galerius
A.D. 300	305–6 Constantius I Chlorus	303 Base of decennalia	
	306–11 Galerius	monument	
	306–12 Maxentius		
	312 Battle at the Milvian Bridge		
	312–37 Constantine the Great	307–13 Basilica of Constantine	
	313 Edict of Milan	313–15 Arch of Constantine	
	337–61 Constantius II		
	350–53 Magnentius		325 Council of Nicaea
	361–63 Julian	Silver plate (Augst)	330 Byzantium (renamed Con-
	375 Beginning of Great		stantinople) becomes capital
	Migrations		Edict of toleration
	379–95 Theodosius the Great		
	395 Western and Eastern empires:		391 Destruction of Library at
	Honorius and Arcadius		Alexandria
400			392 Pagan temples closed

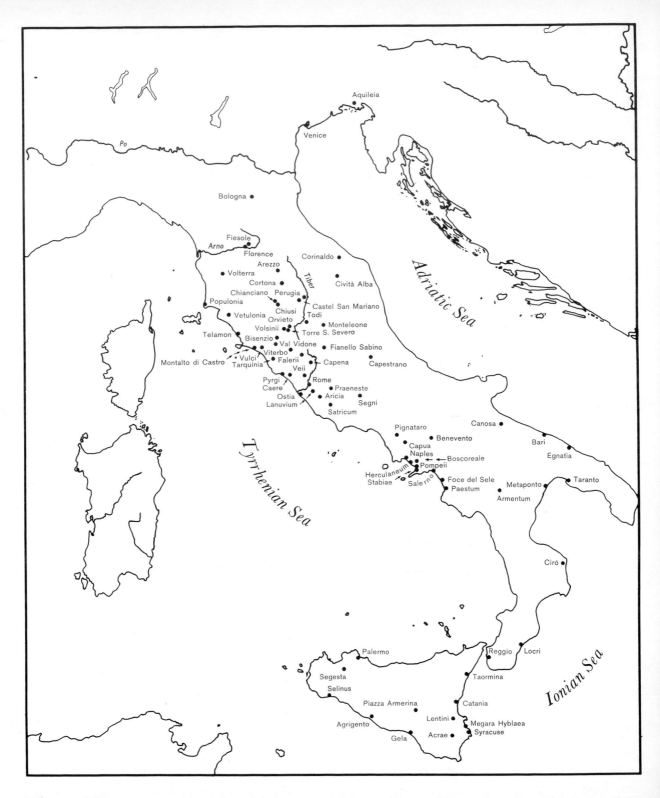

Po

Aquileia

Venice

Bologna

Fiesole

Arno

Florence

Arezzo

Corinaldo

Volterra

Cortona

Tiber

Città Alba

Chianciano   Perugia

Populonia

Chiusi

Castel San Mariano

Vetulonia

Todi

Orvieto

Volsinii

Monteleone

Telamon

Bisenzio

Torre S. Severo

Val Vidone

Fianello Sabino

Viterbo

Montalto di Castro

Vulci

Falerii

Capena

Capestrano

Tarquinia

Veii

Pyrgi

Rome

Caere

Praeneste

Ostia

Aricia

Segni

Lanuvium

Satricum

Pignataro

Canosa

Benevento

Capua

Bari

Naples

Egnatia

Boscoreale

Herculaneum

Pompeii

Stabiae

Foce del Sele

Salerno

Metaponto

Taranto

Paestum

Armentum

Cirò

Adriatic Sea

Tyrrhenian Sea

Ionian Sea

Reggio

Locri

Palermo

Taormina

Segesta

Selinus

Catania

Piazza Armerina

Lentini

Megara Hyblaea

Agrigento

Acrae

Syracuse

Gela

Bibliography

GENERAL WORKS

SICILY AND SOUTHERN ITALY

ASHMOLE, B., *Greek Sculpture in Sicily and South Italy,* London, 1934

BERARD, J., *La colonisation grecque de l'Italie méridionale et de la Sicile dans l'antiquité,* 2d ed., Paris, 1956

BERNABÒ BREA, L., *Musei e Monumenti in Sicilia,* Novara, 1958

BERVE, H., and GRUBEN, G., *Greek Temples, Theaters, and Shrines,* New York, 1963

DUNBABIN, T. J., *The Western Greeks,* Oxford, 1948

FRANKE, P. R., *Die griechische Münze,* Munich, 1964

GUIDO, M., *Sicily: An Archaeological Guide,* London, 1967

JANTZEN, U., *Bronzewerkstätten in Grossgriechenland und Sizilien,* Berlin, 1937

LANGLOTZ, E., *Ancient Greek Sculpture of South Italy and Sicily,* New York, 1965

MATT, L. VON, *Das antike Sizilien,* Zurich, 1959

MATT, L. VON, and ZANOTTI-BIANCO, U., *Grossgriechenland,* Würzburg, 1961

PACE, B., *Arte e civiltà della Sicilia antica,* Milan, 1935–49, 4 vols.

WOODHEAD, A. G., *The Greeks in the West,* New York, 1962

WUILLEUMIER, P., *Tarente des origines à la conquête romaine,* Paris, 1939

ROME

ANDREAE, B., *Architektur im antiken Rom,* Würzburg, 1958

ARIAS, P. E., *La scultura romana,* Messina, 1943

BECATTI, G., *The Art of Ancient Greece and Rome,* New York, 1967

BIEBER, M., *The History of the Greek and Roman Theater,* Princeton, 1961

BOETHIUS, A., *The Golden House of Nero,* Ann Arbor, 1960

BORDA, M., *La pittura romana,* Milan, 1958

BRILLIANT, R., *Gesture and Rank in Roman Art,* New Haven, 1963

BROWN, F. E., *Roman Architecture,* London, 1961

CHARLES-PICARD, G., *L'art romain,* Paris, 1962

CHARLES-PICARD, G., *Living Architecture: Roman,* New York, 1966

CHARLESTON, R. J., *Roman Pottery,* London, 1955

COURBAUD, E., *Le bas-relief romain à représentations historiques,* Paris, 1899

CURTIUS, L., *Das antike Rom,* 3d ed., Vienna and Munich, 1957

ESSEN, C. C. VAN, *Précis d'histoire de l'art antique en Italie,* Brussels, 1960

HANFMANN, G. M. A., *Roman Art,* Greenwich, Conn., 1964

HEINTZE, H. VON, *Römische Porträt-Plastik,* Stuttgart, 1961

JUCKER, H., *Vom Verhältnis der Römer zur bildenden Kunst der Griechen,* Frankfurt, 1950

KÄHLER, H., *The Art of Rome and Her Empire,* New York, 1963

KÄHLER, H., *Rom und seine Welt,* Munich, 1958–60, 2 vols.

KASCHNITZ VON WEINBERG, G., *Römische Kunst,* Hamburg, 1961–63, 4 vols.

KOCH, H., *Römische Kunst,* 2d ed., Weimar, 1949

KRAUS, T., *Das römische Weltreich,* Berlin, 1967

LEVI, M. A., *Roma antica,* Turin, 1963

LÜBKE, W., et al., *Die Kunst der Römer,* Vienna, 1958

MAIURI, A., *Roman Painting,* Geneva, 1953

NASH, E., *Pictorial Dictionary of Ancient Rome,* London, 1961, 2 vols.

NEPPI MODONA, A., *Gli edifici teatrali greci e romani,* Florence, 1961

POLLITT, J. J., *The Art of Rome,* Englewood Cliffs, N. J., 1966

RICHTER, G. M. A., *Ancient Italy,* Ann Arbor, 1955

ROBERTSON, D. S., *A Handbook of Greek and Roman Architecture,* 2d ed., Cambridge, 1959

SCHEFOLD, K., *Römische Kunst als religiöser Phänomen,* Hamburg, 1964

STENICO, A., *Roman and Etruscan Painting,* New York, 1963

STRONG, E. D., *Roman Imperial Sculpture,* London, 1961

TECHNAU, W., *Die Kunst der Römer,* Berlin, 1940

TOYNBEE, J. M. C., *Art in Britain under the Romans,* Oxford, 1964

TOYNBEE, J. M. C., *The Art of the Romans,* London, 1965

VERMEULE, C. C., *European Art and the Classical Past,* Cambridge, Mass., 1964

WHEELER, R. E. M., *Roman Art and Architecture,* New York, 1965

WICKHOFF, F., *Römische Kunst (Die Wiener Genesis),* Berlin, 1912

ZSCHIETZSCHMANN, W., *Die hellenistische und römische Kunst,* Potsdam, 1939

ETRUSCAN ART

BANTI, L., *Il mondo degli Etruschi,* Rome, 1960

BEAZLEY, J. D., *Etruscan Vase-Painting,* Oxford, 1947

BLOCH, R., *Etruscan Art,* Greenwich, Conn., 1966

BLOCH, R., *The Etruscans,* New York, 1958

BOETHIUS, A., et al., *Etruscan Culture: Land and People,* New York, 1963

BROWN, W. L., *The Etruscan Lion,* Oxford, 1960

BRUNN, H., and KÖRTE, G., *I rilievi delle urne etrusche,* Berlin and Rome, 1870–1916, 3 vols. in 4

CLES-REDEN, S. VON, *The Buried People,* New York, 1955

DEMUS-QUATEMBER, M., *Etruskische Grabarchitektur,* Baden-Baden, 1958

DOHRN, T., *Grundzüge etruskischer Kunst,* Baden-Baden, 1958

DUCATI, P., *Storia dell'arte etrusca,* Florence, 1927, 2 vols.

GERHARD, E., *Etruskische Spiegel,* Berlin, 1843–97, 5 vols.

257

GIGLIOLI, G. Q., *L'arte etrusca*, Milan, 1935

GOLDSCHEIDER, L., *Etruscan Sculpture*, New York, 1941

HANFMANN, G. M. A., *Etruskische Plastik*, Stuttgart, 1956

HERBIG, R., *Götter und Dämonen der Etrusker*, Mainz, 1965

HUS, A., *The Etruscans*, New York, 1961

LEISINGER, H., *Malerei der Etrusker*, Stuttgart, 1954

MANSUELLI, G. A., *The Art of Etruria and Early Rome*, New York, 1965

MATT, L. VON, et al., *The Art of the Etruscans*, New York, 1970

MORETTI, M., *Nuovi monumenti della pittura etrusca*, Milan, 1966

PALLOTTINO, M., *Art of the Etruscans*, New York, 1955

PALLOTTINO, M., *Etruscan Painting*, Geneva, 1952

RICHARDSON, E. H., *The Etruscans: Their Art and Civilization*, Chicago and London, 1964

RIIS, P. J., *An Introduction to Etruscan Art*, Copenhagen, 1953

RIIS, P. J., *Tyrrhenika: An Archeological Study of the Etruscan Sculpture in the Archaic and Classical Periods*, Copenhagen, 1941

SANTANGELO, M., *Musei e monumenti etruschi*, Novara, 1958

TEITZ, R. S., *Masterpieces of Etruscan Art* (cat.), Worcester, Mass., 1967

VACANO, O.-W. VON, *Die Etrusker: Werden und geistige Welt*, Stuttgart, 1955

VAN BUREN, E. D., *Figurative Terra-cotta Revetments in Etruria and Latium in the 6th and 5th Centuries* B.C., London, 1921

WEEGE, F., *Etruskische Malerei*, Halle, 1921

THE EARLIEST PERIOD

AKERSTRÖM, A., *Der geometrische Stil in Italien*, Lund and Leipzig, 1943

ALTHEIM, F., *Der Ursprung der Etrusker*, Baden-Baden, 1950

BERNABÒ BREA, L., *Sicily Before the Greeks*, New York, 1958

BIANCOFIORE, F., *La civiltà micenea nell'Italia meridionale, I: La ceramica*, Rome, 1963

CURTIS, C. D., *The Barberini Tomb* (Memoirs of the American Academy in Rome, V), Rome, 1925

CURTIS, C. D., *The Bernardini Tomb* (Memoirs of the American Academy in Rome, III), Rome, 1919

GJERSTAD, E., *Early Rome*, Lund, 1953–66, 4 vols.

GRENIER, A., *Bologne villanovienne et étrusque*, Paris, 1942

HAMPE, R., and SIMON, E., *Griechische Sagen in der frühen etruskischen Kunst*, Mainz, 1964

HULS, Y., *Ivoires d'Etrurie*, Brussels and Rome, 1957

MÜHLESTEIN, H., *Die Kunst der Etrusker: Die Ursprünge*, Berlin, 1929

MÜLLER-KARPE, H., *Vom Anfang Roms*, Heidelberg, 1959

MÜLLER-KARPE, H., *Zur Stadtwerdung Roms*, Heidelberg, 1962

PARETI, L., *La tomba Regolini-Galassi del Museo Gregoriano Etrusco e la civiltà nell'Italia centrale nel secolo VII a. C.*, Vatican City, 1947

RANDALL-MACIVER, D., *Villanovians and Early Etruscans: A Study of the Early Iron Age in Italy*, Oxford, 1924

TAYLOUR, W., *Mycenean Pottery in Italy and Adjacent Areas*, Cambridge, 1958

ARCHAIC ART

BARTOCCINI, R., et al., *Tarquinia: La tomba delle Olimpiadi*, Milan, 1959

BIANCHI BANDINELLI, R., *Le pitture delle tombe arcaiche a Chiusi*, Rome, 1939

DE MARINIS, S., *La tipologia del banchetto nell'arte etrusca arcaica*, Rome, 1961

DUCATI, P., *Le pitture della tomba delle leonesse e dei vasi dipinti*, Rome, 1937

GRIFFO, P., and MATT, L. VON, *Gela: The Ancient Greeks in Sicily*, Greenwich, Conn., 1968

HUS, A., *Recherches sur la statuaire en pierre étrusque archaïque*, Paris, 1961

KRAUSS, F., *Paestum: Die griechischen Tempel*, Berlin, 1943

LEISINGER, H., *Les peintures étrusques de Tarquinia*, Lausanne, 1953

MORETTI, M., *Tarquinia: La tomba della nave*, Milan, 1961

ROMANELLI, P., *Le pitture della tomba della caccia e pesca*, Rome, 1938

VAN BUREN, E. D., *Archaic Fictile Revetments in Sicily and Magna Graecia*, London, 1923

THE FIFTH AND FOURTH CENTURIES B.C.

CAMBOTOGLOU, A., and TRENDALL, A. D., *Apulian Red-Figured Vase-Painters of the Plain Style*, New York, 1961

HAFNER, G., *Ein Apollon-Kopf in Frankfurt und die Niobiden-Gruppe des 5. Jahrhunderts: Griechische Kunstwerke aus Rom*, Baden-Baden, 1962

KLUMBACH, H., *Tarentinische Grabkunst*, Tübingen, 1937

LULLIES, R., *Griechische Bildwerke in Rom*, Munich, 1954

SCHMIDT, M., *Der Dareiosmaler und sein Umkreis*, Münster, 1960

SICHTERMANN, H., *Griechische Vasen in Unteritalien aus der Sammlung Jatta in Ruvo*, Tübingen, 1966

TRENDALL, A. D., *Paestan Pottery*, Rome, 1936

TRENDALL, A. D., *The Red-Figured Vases of Lucania, Campania and Sicily*, Oxford, 1967, 2 vols.

WUILLEUMIER, P., *Le trésor de Tarente*, Paris, 1930

THE THIRD TO FIRST CENTURIES B. C.

BERNARDINI, M., *Vasi dello stile di Gnathia: Vasi a vernice nera*, Lecce, n. d.

BULLE, H., *Eine Skenographie*, Berlin, 1934

CURTIUS, L., *Die Wandmalerei Pompejis*, Leipzig, 1929

DAWSON, C. M., *Romano-Campanian Mythological Landscape Painting*, Rome, 1965

DRÄYER, W., and SCHEFOLD, K., *Pompeji: Zeugnisse griechischer Malerei*, Munich, 1958

GABRIEL, M. M., *Masters of Campanian Painting*, New York, 1952

GREIFENHAGEN, A., *Beiträge zur antiken Reliefkeramik*, Berlin, 1963

HERBIG, R., *Die jüngeretruskischen Steinsarkophage*, Berlin, 1952

KÄHLER, H., *Der Fries vom Reiterdenkmal des Aemilius Paullus in Delphi*, Berlin, 1965

KÄHLER, H., *Seethiasos und Census: Die Reliefs aus dem Palazzo Santa Croce in Rom*, Berlin, 1966

LAVIOSA, C., *Scultura tardo-etrusca di Volterra*, Florence, 1964

LEHMANN, P. W., *Roman Wall-Painting from Boscoreale*, New York, 1953

LULLIES, R., *Vergoldete Terrakotta-Appliken aus Tarent*, Heidelberg, 1962

MAIURI, A., *Ercolano: I nuovi scavi (1927–58)*, Rome, 1958

MERCKLIN, E. VON, *Antike Figurenkapitelle*, Berlin, 1962

PAGENSTECHER, R., *Die Calener Reliefkeramik*, Berlin, 1909

PERNICE, E., *Die hellenistische Kunst in Pompeji*, Leipzig, 1912–41, 7 vols.

PETERS, W. J. T., *Landscape in Romano-Campanian Mural Painting*, Rome, 1965

SCHEFOLD, K., *Pompejanische Malerei: Sinn und Ideengeschichte*, Basel, 1952

SCHEFOLD, K., *Die Wände Pompejis*, Berlin, 1957

SCHWEITZER, B., *Bildniskunst der römischen Republik*, Leipzig, 1948

VESSBERG, O., *Studien zur Kunstgeschichte der römischen Republik*, Lund and Leipzig, 1941

THE EARLY EMPIRE

BUDDE, L., *Ara Pacis Augustae*, Hanover, 1957

HAMBURG, P. G., *Studies in Roman Imperial Art*, Uppsala, 1945

KÄHLER, H., *Die Augustusstatue von Primaporta*, Cologne, 1959

KRAUS, T., *Die Ranken der Ara Pacis*, Berlin, 1953

MAGI, F., *Il ripristino del Laocoonte*, Vatican City, 1960

MORETTI, G., *Ara Pacis Augustae*, Rome, 1948

RIZZO, G., *Le pitture della casa di Livia*, Rome, 1936

SIMON, E., *Ara Pacis Augustae*, Tübingen, 1967

SIMON, E., *Die Portlandvase*, Mainz, 1957

STENICO, A., *La ceramica arretina*, Milan, 1960–66, 2 vols.

STRONG, E. S., *La scultura romana da Augusto a Costantino, I: Da Augusto a Traiano*, Florence, 1923

TOYNBEE, J. M. C., "The Ara Pacis Reconsidered and Historical Art in Roman Italy" in *Proceedings of the British Academy*, XXXIX, 1954, pp. 67–95

ZANKER, P., *Forum Augustum: Das Bildprogramm*, Tübingen, 1968

THE MIDDLE EMPIRE

AURIGEMMA, S., *Villa Adriana*, Rome, 1961

BECATTI, G., *La colonna coclide istoriata*, Rome, 1960

BECATTI, G., *Colonna di Marco Aurelio*, Milan, 1957

BLANKENHAGEN, P. H. VON, *Flavische Architektur und ihre Dekoration untersucht am Nervaforum*, Berlin, 1940

CAPRINO, C., et al., *La colonna di Marco Aurelio*, Rome, 1955

GIULIANO, A., *Il commercio dei sarcofagi attici*, Rome, 1962

GROSS, W. H., *Bildnisse Trajans*, Berlin, 1940

HASSEL, F. J., *Der Trajansbogen in Benevent: Ein Bauwerk des römischen Senates*, Mainz, 1966

KÄHLER, H., *Hadrian und seine Villa bei Tivoli*, Berlin, 1950

PALLOTTINO, M., *L'Arco degli Argentari*, Rome, 1946

PARLASCA, K., *Mumienporträts und verwandte Denkmäler*, Wiesbaden, 1966

ROBERT, C., et al., ed., *Die antiken Sarkophagreliefs*, Berlin, 1890–1966, 5 vols.

SICHTERMANN, H., *Späte Endymion-Sarkophage*, Baden-Baden, 1964

STRONG, E. S., *La scultura romana da Augusto a Costantino, II: Da Traiano a Costantino*, Florence, 1926

TOYNBEE, J. M. C., *The Hadrianic School: A Chapter in the History of Greek Art*, Cambridge, 1934

TUSA, V., *I sarcofagi romani in Sicilia*, Palermo, 1957

WEGNER, M., *Hadrian*, Berlin, 1956

WEGNER, M., *Die Herrscherbildnisse in antoninischer Zeit*, Berlin, 1939

WIRTH, F. W., *Römische Wandmalerei vom Untergang Pompejis bis ans Ende des 3. Jahrhunderts*, Berlin, 1934

ZALOSKER, H., *Porträts aus dem Wüstensand: Die Mumienbildnisse aus der Oase Fayum*, Munich and Vienna, 1961

ZWIKKER, W., *Studien zur Markussäule*, Amsterdam, 1941

THE LATE EMPIRE

GIULIANO, A., *Arco di Costantino*, Milan, 1955

KÄHLER, H., *Das Fünfsäulendenkmal für die Tetrarchen auf dem Forum Romanum*, Cologne, 1964

L'ORANGE, H. P., *Art Forms and Civic Life in the Late Roman Empire*, Princeton, 1965

L'ORANGE, H. P., *Studien zur Geschichte des spätantiken Porträts*, Oslo, 1933

L'ORANGE, H. P., and VON GERKAN, A., *Der spätantike Bildschmuck des Konstantinsbogens*, Berlin, 1939

RIEGL, A., *Spätrömische Kunstindustrie*, Vienna, 1927

Index

Achaeans, 9
Aegina, 68
Agate, 193
Agrigento (Acragas)
　Santa Nicola, 240
　Temple F (Temple of
　　Concordia), 105
Agrippa, 227
Agrippina the Elder, 210
Agrippina the Younger,
　210f.
Alexander the Great, 8, 11,
　112, 137f., 169, 186,
　203, 222, 234, 240
Altar, 8, 10, 118, 169, 208,
　220
　Ara Pacis Augustae, 180,
　　190ff., 204
　Ara Pietatis Augustae, 204
Altheim, F., 9
Amazonomachy, 59, 128f.,
　135
Ancus Marcius, 20
Animal figures, 29, 30f.,
　131, 157
　See also Chariot;
　　Hunting
　Bird, 28, 33, 183
　Bird-demon, 164
　Boar, 119, 228, 240
　Bull, 40, 245
　Dog, 66f.
　Duck, 60
　Eagle, 172
　Elephant, 144f.
　Horse, 38, 41, 51, 94,
　　109, 112, 133, 233,
　　240
　Lion, 28, 60, 91, 126, 135
　Pig, 166, 245
　Ram, 126, 166
　Sheep, 207, 245
　Snake, 111, 121
　Stag, 81, 104, 221
　Swan, 164
　Tiger, 182
　Wolf, 93, 137f.
Antiochus, 169
Antonia, 211
Antoninus Pius, 222, 228,
　230f.
Antonio da Sangallo, 168
Apulian art, 118
Aqueduct, 12
Arabia, 203
Arcesilaus, 11, 181
Archaic art, 76, 84, 86, 88,
　186
　Post-archaic, 98

Architects
　Apollodorus of
　　Damascus, 223
　Polycletus, 11, 96, 98
　Vulca, 34, 62
Architecture. *See also*
　Aqueduct; Citadel;
　Palace; Theater;
　Temple
　Antefix, 22, 65, 73, 170
　Arch, 11, 168, 216, 224ff.,
　　228, 234, 241, 248
　Attic, 234
　Columns, 76, 106, 169,
　　186, 202, 213, 223,
　　227f., 230, 236, 245,
　　247, 249
　Corinthian Order, 218
　Cyma, 40
　Frieze, 39, 51, 129, 211,
　　230, 250
　Ionic Order, 218
　Metope, 39, 46f., 59,
　　80f., 155
　Pediment, 76, 99, 152,
　　159, 170f., 227
　Pilaster, 179, 218
　Portico, 202, 227
　Pronaos, 76
　Scaenae frons, 213
　Tetrapylon, 227, 248
　Tuscan Order, 218
Arezzo, 126
Athenians, 109
Athens
　Acropolis, 8
　Parthenon, 8
　Theseum, 105
Attic art, 34
Augst, 250
Augustine, St.
　De Civitate Dei, 9
Augustus, 7, 10f., 107, 178,
　190ff., 203f., 211, 239f.
　Augustus, 196
　Augustus and Roma, 193
　*Augustus with Drusus and
　　Tiberius*, 196
Aurelian, 238, 244
　*Aurelian as a Builder of
　　Rome's City Wall*,
　　244
Aurunci, 9
Ausones, 9

Banqueting scene, 56ff., 87,
　143
Basilica of Constantine,
　see under Rome
Battles, 109, 123
　Scenes, 28, 86, 114, 153,
　　160, 242f., 248.
　　See also Amazons;
　　Duel; Wars
Cannae, 6
Clastidium, 156

Himera, 76
Lake Regillus, 94
Magnesia ad Sipylus, 173
Milvian Bridge, 250
Telamon, 156
Zama, 173
Beneventum (Benevento)
　Trajan's Arch, 225
Bird, *see under* Animal
　figures
Bisenzio, 16
Bologna, 22
　Benacci Tomb, 25
Boscoreale
　Villa, 182
Bronze, 20, 24f., 29, 82, 91
　Age, 13
　Caldron, 24
　Chariot, 51
　Cist, 135
　Coins, 215
　Head, 49, 71, 80, 84f.,
　　111, 139, 151, 177
　Incense stand, 60
　Mirror, 83
　Relief, 51, 227
　Statue, 10f., 15, 20, 42,
　　45, 93, 112, 120, 122,
　　125f., 134, 156, 164
　Urn, 18
　Vase, 32
Bruttians, 9f.
Brutus, Lucius, 9

Caere (Cerveteri), 27, 35,
　41, 48, 56, 126, 133,
　138, 141
　"Tomb of the Painted
　　Lions," 31
　Regolini-Galassi Tomb,
　　28
Caesar, 10, 180f., 209, 234
Caldron, 24
Cameo, 173, 193, 203, 210
Campania, 137, 149
Campanians, 120
Candelabrum, 10, 112, 121,
　216
Canopus
　Temple of Serapis, 228
Canusium (Canosa), 111,
　163
Capestrano, 44
Capua, 36
Caracalla, 9, 238, 241
Carnelian, 84
Carthage, 169
Carthaginians, 8, 76, 80,
　105, 110, 137
Castel San Mariano, 49
Catania, 13
Cato, 7f.
Catulus, Caius
　Lutatius, 162
Caudini, 9
Chalcedony, 82

Chalcidians, 9
Chariot, 7, 49, 51, 216, 220,
　238f., 241.
　See also Quadriga
　Procession of Chariots, 51
Chonaeans, 9
Cicero, 7, 9
Cimbri, 10, 180
Cirò (Punta Alice), 82
Cist, 116, 135
Citadel, 13
Città Alba, 170f.
Classicism, 11f., 222, 228
Claudius, 203f., 210f.
Clay, *see under*
　Terra-cotta
Clusium (Chiusi), 58, 60
　Pania tumulus, 30
Coins, 11, 137, 166, 227
　Denarius, 196
　Sesterce, 215
　Tetradrachm, 109
Commodus, 234f.
Constantine, 11, 239.
　See also Rome
Constantinople, 247
Constantius Chlorus, 239,
　245
Corinaldo, 42
Corinth, 20, 111
Corinthian art, 22, 34
　Columns, 202
　Pilaster, 218
Cretan art, 22
Crispina, 234f.
Crotona, 13
Cult Act, 167
Cyme, 13, 20

Dacia, 203
Dacians, 223f.
"Daidalic" art, 20
Dance, 58. *See also*
　Human figures
Delphi, 76, 220, 232
Dentatus, Manius
　Curius, 139
Dindia Macolnia, 116
Diocletian, 239, 245, 247
Dioscuri, 94, 112, 134, 173.
　See also Rome
Domitian, 203, 216
Drusus, 196, 202, 211
Duel, 51

Egypt, 190, 228
Elymians, 9
Epidaurus, 137
Eretrians, 9
Eumenes II, 173

Fabius Maximus
　Rullianus, 140
Falerii, 123, 150, 159
Falisci, 9
Fannius, M., 140

Fasano, 148
Fibula, 28f.
Filigree ornament, 28
Flamininus, Q., 169
Flavian, 203, 218, 224f.
    See also Rome
Florus, P. Annaeus, 7
Foce del Sele, 39, 59, 112
Frentani, 10
Fresco, see under Wall
    painting
Funerary. See also Urn
    Monument, 236
    Performance, 66f.
    Procession, 30
    Stele, 181

Galba Addressing His
    Soldiers, 215
Galerius, 245. See also
    Salonika
    Galerius Engaged in
        Battle, 248
Gauls, 7, 77, 110, 137
    Defeated Gaul, 156
Gela, 102
Gem, 11, 84, 166.
    See also Cameo
Geometric art, 19f., 25, 33
Germanicus, 203f., 210f.
Geta, 241
Gilding, 104, 121, 160, 199
Gods, see under
    Mythological figures
Gold, 20, 24. See also
    Gilding
    Fibula, 28f.
    Statue, 8, 181
Gracchi, 10, 180
Granite
    Column, 227
Granulation, 28
Griffin, 24, 230

Hadrian, 222, 227f., 250.
    See also Rome; Tivoli
    Hadrian as a Hunter,
        226f.
Heraclides Ponticus, 77
Herculaneum
    "House of the Mosaic of
        Neptune and
        Amphitrite," 217
Hernici, 8
Hero, 101
Herodotus, 220
Hirpini, 10
Human figures
    Athlete, 84
    Bearded Man, 102
    Boxer, 181
    Dancer, 30, 60, 201
    Flutist, 53, 91
    Girl at a Chest, 86
    Girls Running, 59, 155
    Heroic Warrior, 187

Kneeling Girl, 112
Maidens at Their
    Toilet, 116
Men and horses, 30, 52,
    60
Portrait of an Elderly
    Woman, 141
Prisoners, 242f.
Recumbent Symposiast, 57
Reposing Couple, 56, 104,
    130, 178f.
Seated man, 27
Warrior, 15, 20, 30, 44,
    122, 242f., 245
Wrestlers, 67
Hunting, 81, 119, 227, 240,
    246f.
Hunter and Maiden, 119

Incense stand, 60
Inlay, 139, 151
Ionian art, 34, 41, 69, 76, 88
Ionians, 9
Ischia di Castro, 51
Ivory, 8, 24, 27, 30f., 121,
    181
    Statue, 8, 27, 121, 181
    Vase, 30f.

Jugurtha, 181
Julio-Claudian emperors,
    203
    Julio-Claudian Family,
        211

Kore, 55, 69, 73
Kouros, 27, 42ff., 70

Landscape
    Coastal Landscape, 206
    Landscape with Sheep, 207
    Odyssey landscapes, 188f.
    Sacred Landscape, 194
Lanuvium, 82, 123
Legends, 13, 88, 100
Leontini (Lentini), 13, 70f.
Leprignano, 145
Limestone
    Frieze, 129, 186
    Head, 21, 173
    Metope, 41, 46, 80f., 155
    Relief, 160
    Statue, 36, 44, 152
    Temple, 35, 76f., 80, 106
Livia, 178, 211
Livy, 6ff., 137, 166
Lucanians, 9, 110
"Ludovisi Throne," 89, 91
Lugdunum (Lyon), 196

Macedonia, 9, 169
Macstrna, see under
    Servius Tullius
Mandrocles, 43
Marble. See also
    "Ludovisi Throne"

Altar, 190f., 208, 220
Arch, 226, 241, 250
Column, 223f., 230, 249
Frieze, 230
Head, 22, 69, 72, 82, 94,
    107, 123, 132, 176
Relief, 88f., 162, 207,
    224f., 228, 231, 234
Sarcophagus, 114, 130,
    222, 232, 237, 242f.
Statue, 11, 43, 54, 107,
    187, 196, 201
Temple, 180
Tetrapylon, 248
Marcellus, M. Claudius, 6,
    12
Marcomanni, 234, 236
Marcus Aurelius, 250.
    See also Rome
    Equestrian Statue of
        Marcus Aurelius, 233
    Marcus Aurelius
        Distributing Money,
        234
Marius, 10, 180
Maxentius, Marcus Aurelius
    Valerius, 249
Maximian, Marcus Aurelius
    Valerius, surnamed
    Herculius, 239, 245f.
Megara Hyblaea, 36, 43
Megarians, 9
Messenians, 9
Metalwork, 11, 31. See
    also Bronze; Gilding;
    Gold; Silver
Metellus, 181
Milan, 137
Mirror, 55, 83
Mithridates, 180
Mosaic, 11, 169, 182, 217,
    247
Music, musicians, 30, 53,
    91, 157, 160
Mycenaean citadels, 13.
    See also Pottery
    Post-Mycenaean age, 13
Mythological figures
    Achilles, 51, 160, 250f.
    Actaeon, 81, 220
    Aegisthus, 232
    Aeneas and Anchises, 100
    Africa, 242
    Agamemnon, 208
    Ajax, 208
    Amazons, 92, 114, 128f.,
        130f., 135, 154, 228
    Amor, 196
    Amphion, 181
    Amphitrite, 162, 217
    Amycus, 116, 181
    Anchises, 100
    Antiphates, 188
    Aphrodite, 54, 89
    Apollo, 40, 82, 95, 159,
        177, 196, 232

Apollo Belvedere, 177
Arachne, 221
Arethusa, 109
Argonauts, 114
Argonauts Among the
    Bebryces, 116
Argus, 195
Ariadne, 102, 184, 238f.
Ariadne and the Thiasus
    of Dionysus, 171
Artemis, 40, 95, 196, 220
Artemis and Actaeon, 81
Asclepius, 137
Atalante, 119
Athena, 46, 76, 86, 104,
    116, 221
Athena and Enceladus, 121
Aurora, 196
Bebryces, 116
Bellerophon, 102, 125
Biton, 220
Boreas, 104, 116
Caelus, 196
Calchas, 208
Campus Martius, 228
Castor, 94, 112, 134, 168,
    202
Centaurs, 30, 38, 51,
    237ff., 251
Cercopes, 39, 46
Ceres, 242
Cerycaion, 51
Chimaera, 125f.
Chiron, 251
Cleobis and Biton, 220
Clytemnestra, 232
Concordia, 242
Creon, 111
Cydippe, 220
Demons, 164, 180
Diana, 88, 95
Diana Nemorensis, 71
Dionysus, 158, 171, 184
Dionysus and Ariadne
    on Naxos, 238f.
Dionysus Riding the
    Tiger, 182
Dirce, 181
Electra, 209
Enceladus, 86, 121
Erato, 252
Erechtheus, 104
Eros, 112, 182
Europa Riding the
    Bull, 41
Furies, 232
Galatea, 195
Giant, 169
Goddesses, 36, 48, 54f.,
    68f., 108, 132, 173,
    176, 199, 221, 250
Gods, 9, 72, 162, 164, 220
Hades, 152, 180
Hecuba, 175
Hera, 35, 39, 59, 77, 105,
    112, 220

Heracles, 40, 62, 65, 83, 128, 161, 173, 219
Heracles and the Cercopes, 39
Heracles Seizing a Maiden, 83
Hermes, 51, 195
Hesperides, 219
Hippolytus, 240
Io, 195
Iphigenia, 208
Jason, 111, 131, 164
Juno, 74
Juno Sospita, 82, 123
Jupiter, 168, 181, 245
Laestrygones, 188
Laocoön, 198
Leto, 40
Maenads, 86, 158, 238f.
Mars, 122, 166, 220, 234f., 245
Medea's Revenge, 111
Medusa, 91, 174
Meleager, 119
Menelaus, 208
Mercury, 123
Minerva, 64, 221
Nereid, 118, 160, 162, 212
Nereid Riding a Sea Centaur, 237
Nereid Riding a Sea Dragon, 163
Nereid Riding a Sea Horse, 212
Nike, 116
Niobe, 95f.
Niobid, 96
Odysseus, 30, 189, 251
Oistrus, 111
Orestes, 209, 232
Orithyia, 104
Orpheus Surrounded by the Animals, 157
Paris, 175
Pegasus, 125
Pelias, 131
Persephone, 68, 152
Perseus and Medusa, 91
Perseus Slaying Medusa, 46
Phaedra, 240
Plutus, 200
Pollux, 94, 112, 134, 168, 202
Polydeuces, 116, 181
Polyphemus, 30, 195
Poseidon, 162
Poseidon and Amphitrite, 217
Remus, 8, 92, 137f.
Roma, 244f.
Romulus, 8, 92, 137f.
Satyrs, 86, 160
Silenus, 65
Silenus Grappling with a Serpent, 120

Sphinx, 21, 40, 48, 55
Tellus, 192, 196
Theseus, 238f.
Theseus Abandoning Ariadne, 102
Thetis, 91
Thetis and Achilles, 51
Tinia, 74, 168
Triton and Nereids, 162
Turan, 54
Tydeus, 84
Venus, 170, 234f.
Venus Libitina, 54
Zephyrus, 164
Zethus, 181
Zeus, 20, 40, 74, 173, 190
Zeus and Hera, 80f.

Naples, 206
Naxos, 13
Nemi, Lake, 71, 88, 92
Nero, 203, 218
Nerva, 220, 225
Novius Plautius, 116
Numa Pompilius, 20
Numismatic art, *see under* Coins
Numismatic artists
  Cimon, 109
  Euainetus, 109
  Phrygillus, 109

Ogulnius, G., 137f.
Ogulnius, Q., 137f.
Olympia, 16
  Temple of Zeus, 20, 77ff., 99
Ortiz, G., 20
Orvieto, 32
Ostia, 235

Paestum, 39, 57f.
  "Italic Temple," 155
  Temple of Athena, 76
  Temple of Hera, 35, 77, 105
  Treasury, 39
Painters
  Apelles, 11
  Damophilus, 77, 92
  Gorgasus, 77, 92
  Theorus, 232
  Zeuxis, 238f.
Paintings, 6, 8, 76f., 114, 119, 181, 195, 223
  Battle of Alexander the Great, 169
  Illusionistic architectural painting, 183, 195, 215
Palazzolo Acreide (Acrae), 174
Palermo, 166
Palestine, 216
Palestrina (Praeneste), 28, 116

"Bernardini Tomb," 24, 29
Parthians, 196, 248
Patroclus, 142
  Patroclus' Shade, 147
Paulus, Lucius Aemilius, 169
Pausanias, 20, 222
Pentri, 10
Peperino, 157, 230
Pergamon, 169, 173, 175
Perugia
  Porta Marzia, 168
Phalaris of Acragas, 34
Phocaeans, 9
Piazza Armerina, 246
Picenum, 42, 44
Pithecusa, 13
Plate, 144, 200, 251
Pliny, 8, 11, 77
Plutarch, 6f., 180
Poetry, 136, 148
Poets
  Aeschylus, 76
  Andronicus, Livius, 137
  Bacchylides, 76
  Caecilius, 137
  Ennius, 137
  Goethe, J. W. v., 166, 241
  Homer, 188f.
  Horace, 8, 190
  Lucullus, 181
  Ovid, 190
  Pindar, 76, 105
  Plautus, 137
  Porcius Licinus, 6
  Tertullian, 8
  Virgil, 7, 190, 198
Polledrara necropolis, *see under* Vulci
Pollio, Gaius Asinius, 181
Pompeii, 120, 144, 169, 180f., 195, 206
  "House of the Faun," 182
  "House of Figured Capitals," 179
  House of Lucretius Fronto, 204
  House of the Vettii, 215
  "Villa of the Mysteries," 184
Pompey, 10, 180
Porphyry, 247
Portraiture, 11, 111, 126, 139, 141, 143, 234f., 239, 247
Pottery. *See also* Vase
  Apulian, 110f., 131, 136, 148, 203f.
  Attic, 83, 102, 110
  Bucchero, 31
  Caeretan, 41, 66f.
  Campanian, 110
  Lucanian, 110
  Mycenaean, 13
  Proto-Corinthian, 20, 35

Samian, 8
Pyrrhus, 8, 137, 144
Pythagoras, 76, 89
Pyxis, 17, 30f., 33, 163

Quadriga, 11, 46, 109

Raeti, 196
Ramtha Huzcnai, 114
Relief, *see under* Altar;
  Arch; Bronze; Candelabrum; Column;
  Fountain; Frieze;
  Limestone;
  "Ludovisi Throne";
  Marble;
  Marcus Aurelius'
  Column; Metope;
  Mirror; Pottery;
  Stucco; Terra-cotta;
  Tetrapylon; Trajan's
  Column; Urn; Vase
Repoussé work, 16, 49, 104
Rhegium, 13
Riedesel, J. v., 240
Rome, 93, 156, 162, 232
  Antemnae, 150
  Arch of Constantine, 224, 226f., 234, 250
  "Arch of Portugal," 228
  Arch of Septimius Severus, 241
  Arch of Titus, 216
  Basilica of Constantine, 249
  Cancelleria, 220
  Capitol, 34, 65, 73, 173, 181, 233
  Colosseum, 218
  Equestrian Statue of Marcus Aurelius, 233
  Esquiline, 17, 19, 33, 51, 65, 89f., 92, 96, 140, 147, 153, 188, 218
  Flavian Palace, 219
  Forum Romanum, 26, 45, 47, 52, 94, 107, 118, 170, 202, 216, 241
  Forum of Trajan, 203, 223f., 250
  Forum Transitorium, 221
  Largo Argentina, 176
  Lungotevere in Augusta, 190
  Marcus Aurelius' Column, 236
  Palatine, 51, 73, 150, 219
  "House of the Griffins," 184
  "House of Livia," 195f.
  Pantheon, 226f.
  Porta Latina, 242
  Porta Tiburtina, 157
  Portrait of a Roman, 139
  Prima Porta, 197

Roman Senate, Populace,
  and Soldiers, 220
San Lorenzo in Miranda,
  230
Santa Maria in
  Aracoeli, 125
Sant'Omobono, 62, 64
Scipio's tomb, 136
Temple of Apollo, 95
Temple of Ceres, 77
Temple of the Dioscuri,
  94, 102
Temple of Divus
  Hadrianus, 231
Temple of Faustina, 230,
  234
Temple of Jupiter, 34, 65,
  73
Trajan's Column, 223,
  236
Via Appia, 136
Via Cassia, 220, 244
Via Nazionale, 181
Via Tiburtina, 242
Villa Farnesina, 194
Villa Medici, 204
Villa Torlonia, 142, 147

Sabina
  Consecratio, 228
Sabines, 7f.
Salonika
  Arch of Galerius, 248
Samnites, 8, 10, 110, 120,
  139, 169
Sandstone, 39, 59
  Head, 22
Sarcophagus, 11, 56, 114,
  128, 130, 136, 154, 160,
  222, 232, 239f., 242f
Sardonyx, 172, 203, 210
Sarmatians, 236
Sarsina, 137
Satricum, 74
Schist, 219
Scipio, Lucius Cornelius,
  169
Scipio Africanus, Publius
  Cornelius, 169, 173
Scipio Barbatus, Lucius
  Cornelius, 136
Sculptors
  Agasias, 186
  Agesander, 198
  Apollonius, 181
  Athenodorus of
    Rhodes, 198
  Cleomenes, 11, 208
  Damophilus, 77, 92
  Dositheus of
    Ephesus, 186
  Gorgasus, 77, 92
  Leochares, 123
  Lysippus, 110, 119, 134

Menelaus, 209
Michelangelo, 233
Pasiteles, 11, 181, 209
Phidias, 8, 228
Polycletus, 11, 96, 98
Polydorus, 198
Scopas, 164
Stephanus, 209
Tauriscus, 11, 181
Vulca, 34, 62
Sculpture, 6, 8, 11, 77, 110,
  134.
  See also Bronze;
  Human figures;
  Ivory; Kore; Kouros;
  Limestone; Marble;
  Metope; Relief;
  Sarcophagus; Terra-
  cotta
Seascape, 61
Segesta
  Temple at, 105f.
Seleucus, 194
Selinus
  Temple at, 41
  Temple C, 46f.
  Temple E, 80f.
Septimius Severus,
  see under Rome
Servius Tullius
  (Macstrna), 34, 142
Shield, 16, 25
Sicani, 9
Sicily, 6, 13, 34, 76.
  See also Taormina
Siculi, 9
Signia (Segni)
  Temple at, 74
Silver, 20, 24
  Coins, 109, 196
  Head, 104
  Plate, 200, 251
  Vase, 11, 104, 119
Sombrotidas, 43
Stabiae, 212
Strabo, 7
Stucco, 35, 77, 80f., 105,
  182, 184, 194, 206
Sulla, 10, 180f.
Syracuse, 6, 12f., 69, 109,
  166

Taormina
  Theater, 213
Tarentum (Taranto), 13, 47,
  68, 95, 101, 107f., 129,
  131f., 137, 160, 164,
  171, 179
  Theater, 111
Tarquinia, 60, 108, 114, 154
  "Tomb of the
    Augurs," 66f.
  "Tomb of the Baron," 53
  "Tomb of Hades," 143

"Tomb of Hunting and
  Fishing," 61
"Tomb of the Leopards,"
  86f.
"Tomb of Typhon," 169,
  180
Tarquinian kings, 9, 34, 92
Tarquinius Priscus, 20
Tarquinius Superbus, 34
Temple, see under Caere;
  Canopus; Olympia;
  Paestum; Rome;
  Segesta; Selinus;
  Signia; Veii
Terra-cotta
  Altar, 118
  Bust, 141
  Head, 47, 62, 64, 69,
    73f., 96, 123, 125, 133,
    138, 147, 150, 159,
    164, 175
  Pediment, 171
  Plaque, 48
  Plate, 144
  Relief, 51f., 86, 160, 244
  Statue, 56, 62, 92, 99f.,
    102, 126, 149
  Urn, 14, 60, 178
  Vase, 14, 19, 33, 35, 102,
    131, 136, 144, 148, 161
Teutons, 10, 180, 244
Theater, 180f. See also
  Rome; Taormina;
  Tarentum
  Scene at the Theater, 131
Thessalians, 9
Thurii, 102, 110
Tiberius, 196, 202ff., 211
Timanthes, 208
Titus, 218
  Triumphal Procession
    of Titus, 216
Tivoli
  Hadrian's Villa, 228
Tombs, 22, 126, 162.
  See also Bologna;
  Caere; Paestum;
  Palestrina; Tarquinia;
  Vetulonia; Vulci;
  Wall painting
Trajan, 203, 222, 239, 250.
  See also Beneventum;
  Rome
  Trajan's Battle with the
    Dacians, 224
Tralles, 181
Triclinium, 228
Tripod, 91
Troezenians, 9
Trojans, 142, 147, 203
Troy, 9, 13, 100, 198
Tuder (Todi), 122f.
Tufa, 136, 158, 179
Tullus Hostilius, 20
Tyrants, 10, 34, 76

Umbria, 137
Umbrians, 9, 13
Urartu, 24
Urn, 14, 18, 58, 60, 162,
  168, 178

Val Vidone, 126
Varro, 9, 181
Vase
  Amphora, 35, 199
  Askos, 15
  Bowl, 119
  Calyx-crater, 131, 148
  Cantharus, 160f.
  Cup, 19
  Flask, 136
  Hydria, 41, 66f.
  Portland, 199
  Red-figure, 110
  Stamnos, 102
  Volute-crater, 111
Vase painting, 83, 102, 110,
  125, 131, 203
Veii, 34, 74, 96, 99f., 102
  Temple, 62
Velcha, Arnth, 143
Velcha, Velia, 143
Velletri, 51
Velthur Partunus, 154
Venice
  St. Mark's, 247
Vespasian, 215f., 218
Vetulonia
  Pietrera tomb, 21
Vevzna family, 126
Vibenna, Caelius, 142
Villanova, 13ff., 20, 28f.
Vindelici, 196
Vipinas, Calle, 142
Volsci, 7f., 74
Volterra, 72, 178
Votive offerings, 112, 122,
  125, 133, 164, 194
Vulci, 13, 29, 38, 60, 130,
  135
  "François Tomb," 142,
    147
  Polledrara necropolis, 36
  "Tomb of the
    Inscriptions," 128
  "Tomb of Isis," 36

Wall painting, 11, 53, 58,
  60f., 66f., 87, 120, 140,
  142, 147, 153, 186, 194
Wars, 10, 180, 223, 244.
  See also Battles
  Civil, 10, 110f., 180
  Peloponnesian, 10
  Persian, 10
  Second Punic, 6
  Social, 180
  War Scenes from the
    Samnite War, 140

Photo credits: Alinari, Florence, p. 156 upper, 216, 235. Anderson, Florence, p. 44, 167, 180, 209, 232. E. Böhm, Mainz, p. 35, 36, 40, 43, 46, 69, 77–81, 105, 106, 166, 213, 240, 246. Museum of Fine Arts, Boston, p. 103, 130. Nationalmuseet, Copenhagen, p. 165. Ny Carlsberg Glyptotek, Copenhagen, p. 88. J. Felbermayer, Rome, p. 72. Soprintendenza alle Antichità, Florence, p. 30, 91. Hafner Archives, Mainz, p. 19, 20, 22, 31, 33, 37, 56, 68, 71 (2×), 75, 76, 89, 90, 98, 101, 102, 104, 108, 121 (2×), 149, 151, 154, 173, 176, 178, 179, 181, 186, 187, 194, 199, 201, 202, 207, 211, 215, 217, 218, 220, 223, 225, 230, 231 (2×), 236, 245, 248, 251, Hirmer, Munich, p. 55, 57, 70, 109, 128, 134, 163, 196. Holle Verlag, Baden-Baden, p. 14, 27, 41, 49, 60 (lower), 66/67, 110, 143, 183, 188–90, 204, 214, 227, 233, 247, 249, 250. Badisches Landesmuseum, Karlsruhe, p. 18, 60 (upper), 117, 136. British Museum, London, p. 48, 83, 85, 111. J. Luckert, Berlin, p. 84. Archäologisches Institut, Mainz, p. 28, 132, 155, 203, 222, 234. L. von Matt, Buochs, p. 112, 152, 172. E. Meyer, Vienna, p. 172, 210. Staatliche Antikensammlung und Glyptothek, Munich, p. 120, 162, The Metropolitan Museum of Art, New York City, p. 50. Ashmolean Museum, Oxford, p. 147. M. Pucciarelli, Rome, p. 139, P. Raba, Munich, p. 53, 61, 87, 93, 96, 129, 137, 144, 168, 206, 212, 229, 237, 241–43. G. Rainbird, London, p. 125. Deutsch-Archäologisches Institut, Rome, p. 24, 25 (2×), 29, 39, 42, 54, 59, 82 upper, 86, 94, 95, 97, 100, 118, 119, 123 lower, 126, 146, 156 lower, 158, 160, 175, 191, 192, 205, 208, 219, 221, 224, 226, 228, 238, 239, 244. Gabinetto Fotografico Nazionale, Rome, p. 99, 107 (2×), 142. Museo Provinciale, Salerno, p. 177. Scala, Florence, p. 127, 182, 184. M. Seidel, Mittenwald, p. 13, 15–17, 21, 23, 26, 32, 34, 38, 45, 47, 51, 52, 58, 62 (2×)–65, 73, 74, 92, 113–16, 123 upper, 124, 140, 145, 150, 153, 157, 159, 164, 167, 170, 171, 185, 195, 252. J. Skeel, Ashford, p. 148. J. Tietz, Berlin, p. 161. Musei Vaticani, Vatican City, p. 82 lower, 122, 133 (2×), 135, 138, 141, 142, 197, 198. Kunsthistorisches Museum, Vienna, p. 193, 200, 210. Zwicker, Würzburg, p. 131.

The map was drawn from the author's sketch by J. J. G. M. Delfgaauw, Baden-Baden